The Book of Football Quotations

THE BOOK OF
FOOTBALL
QUOTATIONS

Peter Ball and Phil Shaw

Stanley Paul

London   Melbourne   Auckland   Johannesburg

Stanley Paul & Co. Ltd

An imprint of Century Hutchinson Ltd

Brookmount House, 62–65 Chandos Place, Covent Garden,
London WC2N 4NW

Century Hutchinson Publishing Group (Australia) Pty Ltd
PO Box 496, 16–22 Church Street, Hawthorn, Melbourne, Victoria
3122

Century Hutchinson Group (NZ) Ltd
32–34 View Road, PO Box 40–086, Glenfield, Auckland 10

Century Hutchinson Group (SA) Pty Ltd
PO Box 337 Bergvlei 2012, South Africa

First published 1984
Reprinted 1984
Revised edition 1986

Set in Linotron Times by Input Typesetting Ltd, London

Printed and bound in Great Britain by
R. J. Acford, Chichester, Sussex

British Library Cataloguing in Publication Data

The Book of football quotations.—Rev. ed
1. Soccer—Quotations, maxims, etc.
I. Ball, Peter, *1943–* Shaw, Phil
796.334   PN6084.S6

ISBN 0 09 166161 7

Contents

I just want to get through this trip without being
quoted

BRIAN CLOUGH, with Nottingham Forest in East Berlin,
1980

Acknowledgements

This book would not have existed without the efforts, albeit often unwitting, of hundreds of others. Our first thanks are to the players, managers, officials and fans who made it all possible, and especially to the journalists who waited in the rain at Tottenham, the street at West Brom, or (at least under cover) in the crowded corridor at Anfield to record their 'nanny goats'. They are too numerous to mention, but every reporter for the popular press can take our gratitude as read.

Patrick Barclay, Charles Burgess, Peter Corrigan, Eamon Dunphy, Fred Eyre, Brian Glanville, Geoffrey Green, Frank Keating, David Lacey, David Miller, David Randall, John Roberts and Russell Thomas all contributed with suggestions or material, as did Jeremy Alexander, Roger Alton, Reggie Alton, John Farmer, John Forsyth, Stan Hey, Bob Houston, Simon Kelner, Julie Llewellyn, Ian Ridley, Dave Shaw, Andy Ward and Peter Wilson. David Barber of the Football Association deserves special thanks for guiding us through the FA library.

Sarah Ball, who has lived with wall-to-wall newspapers since we began collecting quotes for *Time Out* in the mid-1970s, tolerated the enterprise with remarkable good humour. And the enthusiasm of Roddy Bloomfield and Marion Paull made us delighted Stanley Paul were our publishers.

Peter Ball and Phil Shaw
June, 1984

Photograph Acknowledgements

Celtic players, *Scottish Daily Record*; Alf Ramsey talking to the England team, Syndication International; Alf Ramsey the player, Fox Photos; Ron Atkinson, Press Association; Marcus Allen and Widnes *v.* Wigan, All-Sport; Frederick Wall and 1974 World Cup panel, unknown; all others by Colorsport

1
The Greats and Others

Players

Steve Archibald

There is still a nagging question surrounding Archie, there is a huge void of uncertainty. Was he good enough or not? A cheat or a Superstar? Or just way beyond our group's thinking?

STEVE PERRYMAN, Spurs captain, in *A Man For All Seasons*, **1985**.

Ossie Ardiles (and Ricardo Villa)

They can't expect to come here and play like fancy flickers. They've joined the toughest league in the world and they'll have to take the knocks. That tackle was to make it clear to him [Ardiles] that he wasn't just playing against a Third Division side. It was to say 'This is a man's League' – and he didn't like it. I think Spurs ought to buy a good stock of cotton wool for such posers. They can't expect not to be tackled just because Argentina won the World Cup.

TOMMY SMITH, former Liverpool hard man, after Swansea *v.* Spurs League Cup tie, **1978**.

Tommy very nice man, very nice player.

OSVALDO ARDILES.

Alan Ball

The only thing that stops me becoming a real world-class player is that I don't score enough goals.

ALAN BALL, **1972**.

I taught football to him not as a game, but as a way of life.

ALAN BALL SENIOR on his son, **1972**.

Gordon Banks

At that moment I hated Gordon Banks more than any man in soccer. But when I cooled down I had to applaud him with my heart. It was the greatest save I had ever seen.

PELE after Brazil *v.* England, Guadalajara, World Cup, **1970**.

Frank Barson (Aston Villa and Wales)

Frank Barson used to keep a little notebook detailing every flick, feint and foul opponents had pulled when playing against him. They never did it a second time, because Barson read and re-read his little storehouse of soccer knowledge as religiously as if it was a bible.

ROY PAUL, Manchester City and Wales, in *A Red Dragon of Wales*, **1956**.

Frank Barson. . .was always the first to admit that he was rough, he was tough, and on occasion the crowd were justified in calling him downright dirty. Barson was also one of the greatest centre-halves football has known.

PETER MORRIS in *Aston Villa*, **1960**.

Jim Baxter

If a poll were to be conducted among them I consider my contemporaries as to who was the greatest Scottish player they ever saw, the outcome would be Jim Baxter. . . . Now if one considers Baxter's game and folklore is your thing, then it will be clear that Scotsmen value things in this world far above success, or integrity or intelligence. What they value most is what Baxter had, they value the completely held conviction of their own superiority.

ALAN SHARP, Scottish novelist and filmwriter, in *We'll Support You Evermore*, **1976**.

In the last minute, with the game won, he took the ball from the Rapid penalty area back towards his own goal, as the Viennese gaped, and when still untackled went back down the left wing with it. Then Walter Skocik went in from behind and Baxter went down. A leg was broken. Typically he said, 'I overdid it.'

JOHN RAFFERTY, soccer journalist, on the Rapid *v*. Rangers match, 1964, in *One Hundred Years of Scottish Football*, **1973**.

Colin Bell

He didn't seem to grasp his own freakish strength. . . . I said to him, 'You are a great header of the ball. You have a terrific shot – and you're the best, most powerful runner in the business. Every time you walk off the pitch unable to say that you were streets ahead of the other twenty-one players, you have failed.'

MALCOLM ALLISON, Bell's manager at Manchester City, **1960s**.

I felt that there was one thing which did upset Malcolm [Allison]. No matter how hard he tried, he could never get as close to Colin Bell as he did to Mike [Summerbee] and Franny [Lee]. They were the champagne set. At the time, Colin Bell was probably the most talked-about player in the country for his world-class potential. Yet instinctively, he was in the black-and-tan brigade with homegrown lads like myself, Alan Oakes and Glyn Pardoe.

MIKE DOYLE, team-mate, **1960s**.

Romeo Benetti

I was at a social function with him the other week, and it's the first time I've got within ten yards of him that he hasn't kicked me. Even then I kept looking over my shoulder. . . .

KEVIN KEEGAN, **1978**.

Mario Bertini

Whenever Bertini came close he managed to dig me in the ribs, or put his fist in my stomach or to kick me in the shins during a tackle. . .he was an artist, I must admit.

PELE on Brazil *v.* Italy, World Cup final, **1970**.

George Best

There are times when you want to wring his neck. He hangs on to the ball when other players have found better positions. Then out of the blue he does something which wins the match. Then you know you're in the presence of someone special.

PAT CRERAND, Manchester United team-mate, in David Meek, *Anatomy of a Football Star: George Best*, **1970**.

Basically, Best makes a greater appeal to the senses than the other two [Finney and Matthews]. His movements are quicker, lighter, more balletic. He offers the greater surprise to the mind and eye. . .he has the more refined, unexpected range. And with it all, there is his utter disregard of physical danger. . . . He has ice in his veins, warmth in his heart, and timing and balance in his feet.

DANNY BLANCHFLOWER, as above.

In six years he has become a cult for youth, a new folk hero, a living James Dean who is a rebel with a cause.

GEOFFREY GREEN, journalist, as above.

The rebel in him is two-fold and contradictory – the creator of a new image for football – yet one who turns back the clock in a search for individual freedom in an age of conformity and method within the game. He is a son of instinct rather than logic.

GEOFFREY GREEN, in *Anatomy of a Football Star: George Best*, **1970**.

The fact that he is a pied piper followed by an ever-growing army worries him not a bit. He is touched mauled and buffeted by the admiring crowd off-stage; he faces an equivalent treatment on the field. Yet, in neither case does he suffer an inflated ego nor a wounded sense of revenge. Like breathing in and breathing out, it is all merely part of the business of life.

GEOFFREY GREEN as above.

The fellow is a football freak. I don't think of him as a small man. I only see those beautiful, tapering muscles and that magnificent style.

JOE MERCER, as above.

'El Beatle'

PORTUGUESE newspaper tribute after Benfica 1, Manchester United 5, **1966**.

He is like a little boy. If anything doesn't go the way he wants, he'll stamp his feet and scream.

JENNIFER LOWE, ex-girlfriend, ex-Miss England, on Best's being sent off in Northern Ireland *v.* Scotland match, in *Anatomy of a Football Star: George Best*, **1970**.

Well, he's got a drink problem, hasn't he?

DON MEGSON, Bournemouth manager, on why Best was left out of his team, **1983**.

I don't care if he's George Best or Pele. Unless he's willing to do hard training, he won't get a look in.

MALCOLM HOLMAN, Ford Open Prison coach, on Best's arrival, **1985**.

I have read all the stories about George's sex life and his drinking bouts and even now I find it difficult to believe most of them. Obviously some of them are true as George has rushed into print on several occasions to tell the world how he jumped in and out of bed and propped up countless bars, though I have a sneaking feelng he was guilty of a bit of blarney at times.

PAT JENNINGS in *An Autobiography*, **1983**.

I was able to stay in my natural environment and develop there as a respected member of the community. If I had been fifteen years old and pulled off the streets of Belfast onto the pitch at Old Trafford, I feel I'd have ended up as George Best has.

BARRY JOHN, Welsh Rugby Union international, **1972**.

Danny Blanchflower

In nine matches out of ten, Blanchflower has the ball more than any two other players on the field – it's an expression of his tremendous ego which is just what a great captain needs.

ARTHUR ROWE, Spurs' manager during 'push-and-run' era, 1950s, in Julian Holland, *Spurs – The Double*, **1961**.

I told Danny it was no use my picking a team on Friday if he was going to change it on the field on Saturday! I had a similar talk with him after the FA Cup semi-final against Manchester City. He sent the right-back forward and moved the man regarded by some as our best forward to right-back.

JIMMY ANDERSON, then Spurs manager, on why he had dropped Blanchflower in 1956, as above.

I don't want to be captain unless I have something to captain.

BLANCHFLOWER on resigning the captaincy after being dropped, as above.

A man and all he believed in was on trial on White Hart Lane's heavy, grassless, March mud-heap. Apart from a single unsuccessful sortie at inside-right, Blanchflower had not been seen in a League match since the previous Christmas. But he played that March day with all the grace and culture that he knew. His every move was positive and constructive and filled with the arts of the game. He disregarded the mud and the slippery ball. He ignored the anxiety of two teams fighting relegation and lifted them up to his own high level.

JULIAN HOLLAND, *Spurs – The Double*, **1961**, on Blanchflower's return to the side in the March 1959 match *v.* Leicester, after being dropped and asking for a transfer in January.

Blanchflower scorned the late and clumsy tackle, eschewed the undirected clearance, forbade the loose pass. With coolness, speed and intelligence, he gauged the finest of interceptions, dribbled the ball or short-passed it out of danger, held it skilfully while his colleagues regrouped, prompted his forwards with careful exact passes.

JULIAN HOLLAND, as above.

In a poor side Danny is an expensive luxury. That's why I dropped him when we had a poor team. But in a good side as Spurs are now he is a wonderful asset through his unorthodox approach and wonderful ball skill.

BILL NICHOLSON, Spurs' 'double' team manager in **1961**, on the time he dropped Blanchflower, as above.

Garry Birtles

For the players he left behind at Manchester United, there will be one lasting memory of Garry Birtles. His weird, way-out gear. . .the fancy bow-ties, winged collars and spectacular suits that nobody else would wear without the courage of four bottles of wine.

STEVE COPPELL, **1982**.

Stan Bowles

The trouble with Bowles is that he falls over as soon as anyone sneezes at him. And a lot of my players have colds.

GEORGE PETCHEY, Orient manager, **1975**.

If Stan Bowles could pass a betting shop like he can pass a ball he'd have no worries at all.

ERNIE TAGG, Crewe manager who rescued Bowles's career after a free transfer from Bury, in **1974**.

Phil Parkes pointed at this stretcher – 'cos I've been off on stretchers plenty of times – and he said, 'Look, Stan, they won't have to run very far to bring you back.' So Malcolm Macdonald chipped in and said, 'There's only one way *I'm* going to be carried off this pitch, and that's shoulder-high.' We drew, no-score, and I think he was brought off before the end of the game.

STAN BOWLES on his England debut, in Sir Alf Ramsey's last match as manager, in Portugal **1974**.

Liam Brady

[He] is often looked on as a great player. He is nothing of the kind. His performance on Wednesday was a disgrace, a monument to conceit adorned with vanity and self-indulgence, rendered all the more objectionable by the swagger of his gait. He was deemed by many observers to have had a splendid game.

EAMON DUNPHY, former Republic of Ireland midfield player, after Ireland 2, Holland 3, Dublin **1983**.

Paul Breitner

I've never met a team which squeal like the Germans. That Breitner especially. Once I put my hand out to hold him off, but he went down screaming as if I'd dropped him one.

BRYAN ROBSON after England *v.* West Germany in World Cup, **1982**.

Billy Bremner

When he makes an easy pass he has his hands flung wide, a theatrical intensity. The crowd think he is posturing, call him 'big head'. In fact, by his balance and concentration he is ensuring absolute accuracy when so many others are too casual over the undemanding.

ARTHUR ROWE in Tony Pawson, *The Football Managers*, **1973**.

Trevor Brooking

Swearing, whether one accepts it or not, is part of the game. Kevin Keegan has written that I never swear and when I do I say something like 'Oh scum'. This is not quite true. I do have a quiet curse at myself sometimes when I make a mistake.

TREVOR BROOKING in *An Autobiography*, **1981**.

Trevor Brooking floats like a butterfly. . .and stings like one. I have never had a high opinion of him as a player. He has been lucky enough to become a member of teams that he shouldn't really have had a sniff at. I believe his lack of application and that of other players like him have meant relegation for West Ham in the past and the failure to win promotion this time.

BRIAN CLOUGH before **1981** FA Cup final. Brooking, whom Clough once tried to buy for Derby, scored the winning goal.

John Charles

Everything John does is automatic. When he moves into position for a goal chance it is instinctive. Watch me and you will see I am seconds late. I do not possess this intuitiveness – I have to work it all out up here [his head]. I work at the skills as hard as I can. But all my thinking has to be done in my head. My feet do not do my thinking for me as they do for a player like John Charles. That is why I can never be as great a footballer as he.

DANNY BLANCHFLOWER in Julian Holland, *Spurs – the Double*, **1961**.

Charles, whom I regard purely and simply as a centre-forward, is not yet in the same class as Tommy Lawton, di Stefano or Dixie Dean. Many good judges think that centre-half is his true position. For me, his tackling does not carry enough 'bite' for a key defender. . . . He does not make enough use of his tremendous physical attributes. Instead, I feel, he likes to play football without bodily contact, which is patently impossible.

STAN CULLIS, Wolves manager of the 1950s, in *All for the Wolves*, **1960**.

Bobby Charlton

I once asked Bobby Charlton for the best way to United's training ground, and I'm still waiting for an answer.

TED MacDOUGALL on his brief and unhappy stay with Manchester United, **1974**.

The fact that they accused Bobby Charlton of sheltering me while I 'stole' a bracelet proves I'm innocent. Bobby has never done a dishonest thing in his life.

BOBBY MOORE on the 'jewel theft' incident in Bogota, **1970**.

Allan Clarke

Greaves was the best of the lot, and certainly in a class of his own in being able to dribble round people, as if they weren't there, to create his own chances. But when it came to actual finishing I'd say Allan was definitely on a par with him. When we had shooting practice at Leicester there were days when I felt almost unbeatable, but Clarkey was probably the only player there who would never be psyched by me. He'd be coming through with the ball and as he hit it, he'd look up as if to say: 'You bloody save that one then.'

PETER SHILTON in Jason Tomas, *The Magnificent Obsession*, **1982**.

I would love to play in England. Leeds I like, because I like Allan Clarke, I like his way of playing.

JOHAN CRUYFF, **1975**.

W. N. (Nuts) Cobbold

Swathed in rubber bandages and ankle-guards he never got crocked. . . . As a dribbler we have never seen his equal. He had a peculiar, shuffling run; just a wriggle between the halves, and a wonderful knack of shooting at quite unexpected moments and impossible angles; and his shooting boots must have been made by Krupp. 'Nuts' had one weakness, and that was his heading; the only time he was ever known to be angry was when outside wingmen persisted in 'middling' high.

C. B. FRY, **1905**.

The Bayard of the football field, the forward without fear and without blame.

C. B. FRY.

George Cohen

We used to say about George Cohen: 'He's hit more photographers than Frank Sinatra.' George was quick and broke up the flanks exceptionally well, but his final ball was rarely on target. Usually he would hit his cross into the crowd, or into the photographers.

BOBBY ROBSON in *Time on the Grass*, **1982**.

Eddie Colman

Sharp as a needle, a brilliant little player. To be honest, I fancied him more than Duncan Edwards.

JOE MERCER.

When he waggled his hips he made the stanchions in the grandstand sway.

HARRY GREGG, Manchester United goalkeeper at **1958** Munich air crash, where 'Snakehips' Colman died.

Denis Compton

I shall not forget my introduction to Denis Compton. The cheerful hand of Britain's Number One Sportsman, the firm grip of his hand, and his cheery 'I'm very pleased to meet you, Bill' were typical of what I expected from this outstanding footballer-cricketer, and later, when we were changing, I had a close-up of the wonderful coolness that might be termed 'Typical Compton'.

BILLY WRIGHT in *Captain of England*, **1950**.

Charlie Cooke

That Cookie. When he sold you a dummy, you had to pay to get back into the ground.

JIM BAXTER, a Scotland team-mate in **1966–67**.

Johan Cruyff

He has shown how far ahead of his time di Stefano was 20 years ago. In many ways they're identical. They operate over the whole length of the pitch, starting attacks yet being there to help conclude them. Cruyff has the same even temperament as di Stefano, but can be hard, and brave when necessary. A super-player.

DETTMAR CRAMER, leading German coach, after **1974** World Cup finals.

Kenny Dalglish

Och, just let him on the park.

JOCK STEIN on whether Dalglish's best position was in attack or midfield.

Kenny calls all his goals 'tap-ins' until we come to the end of the season and we are talking money. Suddenly he changes his mind.

BOB PAISLEY, **1982**.

I play in a country with some of the world's best footballers, but there are players in England who can do as well as Platini. Kenny Dalglish was a better player two years ago than Maradona.

GRAEME SOUNESS, then with Sampdoria, **1986**.

THE GREATS AND OTHERS

The best player this club has signed this century.

JOHN SMITH, Liverpool chairman, **1986**.

The way he sticks out his arms and legs represents plain obstruction. He's supposed to be the best screener of the ball in the game. I say that's rubbish. Too many refs cannot see that it is breaking the law.

CLIVE THOMAS, referee, **1984**.

Peter Doherty

He was the great North Star that twinkled brightly in the heavens, promising untold glory, beckoning me to follow and always showing the way.

DANNY BLANCHFLOWER in Julian Holland, *Spurs – the Double*, **1961**.

Derek Dooley (Sheffield Wednesday)

I have never met a man who had such an eye for the quarter-chance – half-chances Derek regarded as sitters. . . . He was slow to get up speed, but once he did start moving he was like a whole herd of elephants on the rampage.

NEIL FRANKLIN, former Stoke and England centre-half, in *Soccer at Home and Abroad*, **1956**.

Duncan Edwards

The Kohinoor diamond amongst our crown jewels. Even when he had won his first full England cap and was still eligible for our youth team, he used to love turning out at a lower level. He remained an unspoiled boy to the end, his head the same size it had been from the start. He just loved to play anywhere and with anyone.

JIMMY MURPHY, Manchester United assistant manager at time of Munich.

Tom Finney

Tommy Finney was grizzly strong. Tommy could run for a week. I'd have played him in his overcoat. There would have been four men marking him when we were kicking in. When I told people in Scotland that England were coming up with a winger who was better than Stanley Matthews, they laughed at me. But they weren't bloody laughing when Big Georgie Young was running all over Hampden Park looking for Tommy Finney.

BILL SHANKLY.

Although I might sound rather Irish, I would say that Matthews is the greater of the two – but I would prefer to have Finney in my club side if I was forced to pick between them. While Stan has no equal as a ball artist and might make more goals than Finney for his forward colleagues, the Preston man has a greater potential for scoring goals.

STAN CULLIS on the Matthews-Finney debate in *All for the Wolves*, **1960**.

William ('Fatty') Foulke (England goalkeeper)

A football wonder is Willie, the most talked-of player in the World. A Leviathan (22½ stone) with the agility of a bantam. The cheeriest of companions and in repartee as difficult to score against as when between the posts.

WILLIAM PICKFORD and ALFRED GIBSON in *Association Football and the Men who made it*, **1906**.

As a draw alone, Foulke is worth his weight in gold. . . . He stops low 'daisy-cutters' and high dropping shots with equal ease, and his punch dispatches the ball to a distant point on the horizon.

J. T. ROBERTSON, Chelsea manager, in *The Book of Football*, **1906**.

Hughie Gallacher

When I ran out onto the pitch there was suddenly a huge 'Ohhh' of disappointment. The crowd had just noticed how small I was. They thought I was far too wee.

HUGHIE GALLACHER, centre-forward for Scotland's 'Wembley Wizards', on his Newcastle United debut in **1926**.

Archie Gemmill

I have only to think about him to realise nothing is impossible in football.

PETER TAYLOR, **1982**.

Johnny Giles

An incredible player. I thought he was miles better than Bremner. A better passer than Bremner; shrewder, more devious than Bremner; and harder when he wanted to be.

STEVE PERRYMAN, Spurs player, in *A Man For All Seasons*, **1985**.

Andy Gray

His style is more suited to Rugby Union.

UDO LATTEK, Bayern Munich coach, **1985**.

Eddie Gray

When he plays on snow, he doesn't leave any footprints.

DON REVIE, **1970**.

Harry Gregg

If Harry had been in the Falklands he would definitely have been a Colonel H. He's that type, which doesn't normally appeal to us weedy liberal intellectuals, but there was this wonderful humanity about him, and there is no malice in him.

EAMON DUNPHY, Manchester United reserve, 1960s, when Gregg was first-team goalkeeper, **1983**.

> But some who stood by me I did hold high
> Big Greggy was one and him I did respect.
> But now, Harry, I can tell you we were different,
> Cos the burning fires which turned your pages
> Never came to me and that I cannot change.

JOHN FARMER, England Under-23 keeper at Stoke with Gregg.

Billy Hamilton (Northern Ireland)

In another week special stars like Zico, Maradona and Hamilton will have gone home and Spain will be bankrupt.

BARCELONA NEWSPAPER, World Cup finals, **1982**.

Tommy Harmer

He could flick the ball on to his head, nod it back to his foot and keep it balanced one way or another just as long as you were prepared to stand and watch him.

ARTHUR ROWE on the ball-playing Spurs inside-forward of the 1950s, in *The Encyclopedia of Association Football*, **1960**.

Ron Harris

We've played Chelsea ten times, and he's been booked every time for tackles on me. George Best says in his book that all Harris can do is man-to-man mark, and that's right. If you thought, I'll stay with this geezer and wherever he runs, run with him, and just not be distracted. . .there's nothing I could do about it. Imagine what a trained athlete, a man like Harris, can do with his mind set – the ball could be there, two yards away, but all he wants to do is just stay here with me.

STAN BOWLES in **1976**. Harris was later a team-mate at Brentford.

I like to think that apart from being a bit of a butcher, I've something else to offer.

RON HARRIS, **1979**.

Asa Hartford

Asa doesn't give you the ball. He lends it to you for a second or two.

MALCOLM ALLISON, in his second stint as Manchester City manager, **1979**. The same has been said of Ossie Ardiles by Terry Yorath.

Colin Bell hits good balls, but they are straightforward ones, the ones you see are on from the stand. With Asa, he plays the angles and sees little openings which you haven't seen until he does it.

MARTIN BUCHAN, a Scotland team-mate in the **1970s**.

Hartford has never played disciplined football in his life. He will have to here. At Ipswich he kept dashing off to mark Mick Mills. I got a message out to him that if he wanted to meet Mills that badly I could arrange an interview after the game.

BRIAN CLOUGH during Hartford's brief stay at Nottingham Forest, **1979**.

Gordon Hill

The lad we have christened Merlin the Magician. An incredible kid. He is maddening to play with. He gives the ball away. And the ball is precious in football. . .but if you try and instil too much common sense into him, you will destroy his capacity for the spontaneous, the unusual.

EAMON DUNPHY, a Millwall team-mate, in *Only a Game?*, **1976**.

He is a very selfish player. The other lads have had to do a lot of work to accommodate him.

DAVE SEXTON, Manchester United's manager, on selling Hill to Derby, **1978**.

Glenn Hoddle

Hoddle a luxury? It's the bad players who are a luxury.

DANNY BLANCHFLOWER, **1981**.

Hoddle is too tall to be a world-class player.

JOHAN CRUYFF, **1983**.

Roger Hunt

Yes, he misses a few. But he gets in the right places to miss them.

BILL SHANKLY, **1966**.

Norman Hunter

I'm fairly quick tempered, but it's up and down and done. Just for two seconds I really go. The silliest thing I ever did was go after that fellow Rivera in the Cup Winners' Cup at Salonika. He kicked me and I went after him. If he'd been closer I'd have hit him, but he'd walked away. By the time I'd trudged all that distance my temper had gone down again and I didn't want to do anything. I just laid my hands on him and I got sent off.

NORMAN HUNTER, Leeds and England defender, **1973**.

Geoff Hurst

Deep down all the lads will be keeping a sort of score in their heads. Every time they jump for the ball and get it they'll be chalking it down, 'Three to me, one to Geoff Hurst' or whatever. Despite what the boss says he is special. Nicking a ball off a player like that, beating him in a tackle, is something you'll always remember. Magic!

PAUL PRICE, Tividale captain, before Tividale v. Telford cup-tie, 1976–77. The Tividale manager had said that Hurst was just a Southern League player now. Brian James, *Journey to Wembley*, **1977**.

Leighton James

You're very deceptive son – you're even slower than you look.

TOMMY DOCHERTY, then Derby manager.

Pat Jennings

He might be a bit vulnerable to a hard low shot from the edge of the six-yard-box.

DON HOWE, Arsenal coach, 1983.

Somewhere in there the grace of a ballet dancer joins with the strength of an SAS squaddie, the dignity of an ancient king, the nerve of a bomb disposal officer.

EAMON DUNPHY, 1983.

Jimmy Johnstone

On my first day as Scotland manager I had to call off practice after half-an-hour because nobody could get the ball off wee Jimmy Johnstone.

TOMMY DOCHERTY, 1970.

Kevin Keegan

Kevin Keegan is so famous that when we were in the Casbah even the blind men were calling out his name.

LAWRIE McMENEMY, 1983.

Kevin Keegan is the Julie Andrews of football.

DUNCAN McKENZIE, 1981.

To call Keegan a superstar is stretching a point. Skill-wise, there are a lot of better players around. He's not fit to lace my boots as a player.

GEORGE BEST after Keegan claimed Best had contributed to soccer's declining popularity, 1982.

Keegan is not fit to lace Best's drinks.

JOHN ROBERTS, soccer writer, **1982**.

Denis Law

Denis was in the class of di Stefano, because he could do everything, organize a side and score goals. His close control was not as good perhaps, but he beat people by his speed of thought.

HARRY GREGG, Manchester United team-mate, 1960s, in John Motson and John Rowlinson, *The European Cup 1955–80*, **1980**.

He was a man's man who could look after himself on the field, and off it he was a good professional and stood up for what he thought was right. Busby knew how important he was. When Denis was doubtful the boss would practically be on his hands and knees hoping he could play.

HARRY GREGG, as above.

Nat Lofthouse

Lofty the Lion of Vienna
Has retired from t'football field
It took a medical specialist
To make Lofthouse finally yield.

Like a centurion tank was our Nathan
Wi' a turn of speed like bomb
Many a goalie's said sadly
'I wonder where that came from?'

Harry Gregg just after t'final
Went into Nat's for a beer
Who returned his money and told him
We don't charge goalkeepers here.

MR KAY of Tonge Moor, Lancashire, from 'Lofthouse Saga' on the Bolton and England centre-forward's retirement in **1960**.

Malcolm Macdonald

The best overlapping left-back in the country.

RODNEY MARSH.

Jimmy McGrory

Herbert Chapman told me they would paint London to get me. I was very flattered but I had not the slightest intention of leaving Celtic. McGrory of Arsenal would never have sounded as good as McGrory of Celtic.

JIMMY McGRORY on why he turned down a £10,000 transfer to Highbury in **1928**.

Duncan McKenzie

He is like a beautiful motor car. Six owners and been in the garage most of the time.

JOHN TOSHACK, **1978**.

People say that when we're up against it I'm not the man to call on. I accept that, but then I'm not a physical player or a good defender. I tend to fall down when we are under the collar. That's the way I am.

DUNCAN McKENZIE, **1979**.

Billy McNeill

Billy McNeill sets a high standard of conduct for all of us, and this is the main reason why you do not see any long-haired wonders walking through the doors at Celtic Park as playing-staff members of the club. Professional football is our business. We feel we do not have to look like a crowd of discotheque drop-outs to attract attention. I reckon the tidy player off the field will improve the tidiness of his play on the field.

BOBBY MURDOCH, Celtic and Scotland, in *All the Way with Celtic*, **1970**.

Diego Maradona

Watching him on Wednesday I was transported back to bad days with Millwall at Carlisle. You work your tail off for five minutes getting the ball and then this bloke gives it away. Every time he got it it was a flick up into the air, a bicycle kick or a dive. He is the South American Gordon Hill.

EAMON DUNPHY, **1984**.

Pele had nearly everything. Maradona *has* everything. He works harder, does more and is more skilful. Trouble is that he'll be remembered for another reason. He bends the rules to suit himself.

SIR ALF RAMSEY after Maradona's 'handball' goal *v*. England, **1986**.

The best one-footed player since Puskas.

SIR STANLEY MATTHEWS in Mexico City, **1986**.

Rodney Marsh

£200,000 was a lot of money to spend to lose the League championship.

JOE MERCER on Malcolm Allison's signing of Marsh for Manchester City, **1972**.

I believed that Rodney's touch of theatre, his marvellous skill, could be the element which finally snapped United's hold in the city. I suspect that if you asked Manchester City fans today whether I did the right thing in signing Marsh they would answer a firm yes. They have learned to live with his extravagances, his inconsistencies. It is, after all, the inevitable price you pay for the promise of magic.

MALCOLM ALLISON in *Colours of My Life*, **1975**.

Stanley Matthews

How many times have you heard the crowd shout to a defender, 'Go in and tackle him,' when the master-winger is dilly-dallying with the ball? I have on dozens of occasions, but those who have played against Stanley appreciate that it is just what he is encouraging a defender to do. If, incidentally, you ever hear anyone comment that Matthews is a trifle on the slow side, and cannot hit a ball with his left foot, refer them to me.

BILLY WRIGHT, in *Captain of England*, **1950**.

Stan was unique. He never went for 50–50 balls, didn't score many goals, and was not good in the air. But on his day he was unplayable. He beat fellows so easily, with such pace and balance, often taking on four or five at a time.

JOE MERCER in David Meek, *Anatomy of a Football Star: George Best*, **1970**.

You usually knew how he would beat you. You could not do anything about it though.

DANNY BLANCHFLOWER in David Meek, *Anatomy of a Football Star: George Best*, **1970**.

Tha can tell tha father from me that if he fancies chasing Brother Matthews here around for ninety minutes, then I'll swap jobs with tha father anytime and I'll have his wages and he can have mine.

TOMMY BANKS, Bolton and England player of the **1950s**, countering arguments at Professional Footballers' Association (PFA) meeting that, compared to factory workers, footballers were already well paid.

I am told by many that I was the match-winner. But I say that we had eleven match-winners.

STANLEY MATTHEWS in *The Stanley Matthews Story*, **1960**, on the 1953 Blackpool *v*. Bolton FA Cup final.

He was the opposite of glamorous: a non-drinker, a non-smoker, careful with his money, brought up among thrift and the ever-looming threat of dole and debt. . . . He came from that England which had no reason to know that the Twenties were Naughty and the Thirties had style.

ARTHUR HOPCRAFT, in *The Football Man*, **1968**.

If I had to get 'stuck in' to get through a game I'm afraid that my career would have ended long ago.

STANLEY MATTHEWS in *The Stanley Matthews Story*, **1960**.

Joe Mercer

They wouldn't last a postman his morning round.

DIXIE DEAN, **1930s** Everton colleague, on Mercer's spindly, bandy legs.

Bobby Moore

Bobby was great at that. Someone would come and kick a lump out of him, and he'd play as though he hadn't even noticed. But ten minutes later. . .whoof!. . .He had a great 'golden boy' image, Moore. But he was *hard*.

GEOFF HURST, West Ham and England team-mate, 1960s–70s, in Brian James, *Journey to Wembley*, **1977**.

Remi Moses

Half a million for Remi Moses? You could get the original Moses and the tablets for that price!

TOMMY DOCHERTY, **1982**.

Bobby Murdoch

That is his great ability: to be composed on the ball. He isn't fast, he isn't strong in the tackle, he doesn't hit a great long ball, he can't beat a man. But what he is great at, when everyone else in the division is going at ninety miles an hour, hitting impossible balls, trying to squeeze things into spaces when it is just not on, is being composed and slowing it down. Knocking the fifteen-or-twenty yard ball, getting it back, and knocking it again.

EAMON DUNPHY on Murdoch at Middlesbrough in *Only a Game?*, **1976**.

Charlie Nicholas

He gets lots of women after him and when sex is offered on a plate he takes it. He wants to play the field.

SUZANNE DANDO, ex-Olympic gymnast and girlfriend of Nicholas, **1984**.

Hmmmm, Charlie. It seems he's getting a lot of everything except the ball.

JIMMY GREAVES on Nicholas's poor display against Sheffield Wednesday in **1984**, the day Nicholas's revelations about his lifestyle had hit the Sunday papers.

Peter Osgood

I think Peter Osgood has more ability than Tom Finney, and he's got the height, 6ft 2in, and almost everything else. He hasn't quite got the killer instinct around the box but once he overcomes that he could be the greatest.

TOMMY DOCHERTY, his manager at Chelsea, **1966**.

Pele

Pele does everything superbly with the possible exception of taking a dive in an opponent's penalty area. He has to learn about that art, though with his skills I can't think why he bothers to lower himself and start acting.

MARTIN PETERS in *Mexico 70*.

Martin Peters

Martin Peters is a player ten years ahead of his time.

ALF RAMSEY, **1968**.

Martin Peters? He's the one who's ten years ahead of his time, so we've got to wait for him to come good.

MALCOLM ALLISON, **1970**.

Michel Platini

Even his feet are intelligent.

MICHEL HIDALGO, France manager, **1984**.

I analyse the whole situation. I have the chance most often of choosing the right solution and having the skill to apply it. I have a very good right foot and a good little left foot, and I'm not bad with my head either. I can defend, too, if needs.

PLATINI, **1984**.

Ferenc Puskas

His shooting was unbelievable and his left foot was like a hand, he could do anything with it. In the showers he would even juggle with the soap.

FRANCISCO GENTO, Real Madrid team-mate 1950–60s, in Motson and Rowlinson, *The European Cup 1955–80*, **1980**.

Wherever we played in Europe there would be a little group of Hungarians waiting for him. I never knew there were so many Hungarians! He would always give them something – a souvenir or perhaps some money. I'm sure he has no medals left.

GENTO, as above.

He was the only player I used to stay and watch after training.

GENTO, as above.

Alf Ramsey

Ramsey – tha's as much use as a chocolate teapot.

MICHAEL PARKINSON, quoting fan's comment as winger Johnny Kelly skinned Alf
Ramsey – Barnsley *v*. Southampton, **1950s**.

He was one of the best examples of someone who made himself
into a good player. Alf became the dominant character in the
team. But he in particular didn't start that way. He gradually
changed himself to fit the picture. He was an accurate player
naturally and he found it very much easier to play the short game
than in the style of his Southampton days. I didn't teach Alf. He
very soon himself saw the logic and safety of kicking within his
distance accurately. He practised tirelessly and made himself into
a ball player.

ARTHUR ROWE in *The Encyclopedia of Association Football*, **1960**.

Alf was never a great one for small talk when he was with England
parties; football was his one subject of conversation. He was
always a pepper-and-salt man, working out moves and formations
with the cruets on the table.

JACKIE MILBURN, an England team-mate.

To have Alf Ramsey in the England side as my vice-captain was
always a source of inspiration, for the sturdy Spurs right-back was
another of those reliable chaps who'd stand by you all the time.
Never have I heard him complain. His whole being is centred
upon playing good football to beat the opposition.

BILLY WRIGHT, Wolves and England captain, in *Football is my Passport*, **1959**.

John Robertson

He may be thirty and overweight, but he's the only player I've
got who can control a ball.

BRIAN CLOUGH, the day before Robertson joined Peter Taylor at Derby, **1983**.

Ian Rush

Painful to watch, but beautiful.

DAVID PLEAT after Rush had scored five against his Luton side, **1983**.

Bill Shankly

Shanks is getting past it. He's letting the left-half take his own throw-ins.

EVERTON player to Joe Mercer.

Peter Shilton

I've seen forwards get past me with all the confidence of a Pele or a Johan Cruyff and then, faced by 'Shilts', suddenly lose their nerve. I mean, it's happened to me when I've tried to beat him in training. All he has to do is crouch a little bit, and he sort of spreads and fills the bloody goal up.

LARRY LLOYD, in Jason Tomas, *The Magnificent Obsession*, **1982**.

In terms of dedication and the intensity of preparation for his work, Peter Shilton is the equal of Geoff Boycott. But he has an advantage Geoff does not have. Peter is able to have a day at the races or a bloody good drink now and then.

LAWRIE McMENEMY, **1983**.

G. O. Smith (Corinthians and England, 1893–1901)

I remember his chatting about the cleverness of a boy centre-forward and remarking to another boy. . . . 'He's simply great; in fact, another G. O. Smith!' 'Smith,' queried the other, 'who's G. O. Smith?' Young Edgar fixed a stern eye upon his companion as he said, with an air of disgust, 'You don't know G. O. Smith? Good Lord! Go and learn your History of England!'

F. B. DOUGLAS-HAMILTON of Edgar Kail, the Dulwich Hamlet amateur who played for England in 1929, in *The Boy's Own Annual*, **1933–34**.

He knew that football is a manly game, calling for qualities of pluck, grit and endurance, and when he got hurt – as all men do – he never whined or grumbled. He took his courage in both hands, and never funked the biggest back that bore down on him. If not exactly a sprinter few men could run faster with the ball at their toe, and one wondered where he acquired the power that sent the ball whipping into the net like a shot from a gun. To see him walk quietly on to the field with his hands in his pockets, and watch the fine lines of an intellectual face, one wondered why the student ventured into the arena of football. But watch him on the ball with opposing professionals – maybe the best in the land – in full cry after him, and you saw a veritable king among athletes.

PICKFORD and GIBSON, **1906**.

Tommy Smith

The king of 'em all. . .the best pro I've ever met. He must have played about two million six-a-sides in his day. But this morning he'd have fought his best mate over a throw-in.

EMLYN HUGHES, Liverpool team-mate, 1960s–70s, in Brian James, *Journey to Wembley*, **1977**.

Graeme Souness

Souness kicked me. There's no friction on my part, but I always seem to have trouble from him.

TERRY YORATH after Wales *v*. Scotland match, **1979**.

He's the nastiest, most ruthless man in soccer. Don Revie's bunch of assassins at Leeds were bad enough, but there is a streak in Souness that puts him top of the list.

FRANK WORTHINGTON, **1984**.

There is black and white proof I'm not the killer I'm supposed to be. I've only been sent off twice.

SOUNESS, **1985**.

When it was 2–0, Souness amused himself by making fun of us with words and gestures. He may be a great player, but he isn't worth much as a man.

DARIO BONETTI, Roma defender, after defeat by Sampdoria, **1984–5**.

If he was a chocolate drop, he'd eat himself.

ARCHIE GEMMILL, Scotland team-mate, **1978**.

Alfredo di Stefano

He was one of the greatest, if not the greatest footballer I had ever seen. At that time we had forwards and defenders doing separate jobs, but he did everything.

MATT BUSBY in Motson and Rowlinson, *The European Cup 1955–80*, **1980**.

Most of all, he would make us want to win. Whenever we practised, even when we played cards or basketball in the gym, he would want to win. When I became a manager I realized how important it was to have a player like that on the field.

FRANCISCO GENTO, Real Madrid team-mate in six European Cup finals, 1956–62, in *The European Cup 1955–80*.

To ask a man to mark him, is to ask him to commit suicide. It is better to mark the others tightly, and let the artist play.

ALBERT BATTEUX, Reims manager, before the **1959** European Cup final. Real won 2–0, di Stefano scoring. Motson and Rowlinson, *The European Cup 1955–80*.

Nobby Stiles

Andy Lochhead was streaking towards goal when Nobby clipped him from behind. Out came my book and Stiles, full of apologies, pleaded: 'It's the floodlights, ref. They shine in my contact lenses and I can't see a thing.' As I was writing Nobby leaned over and said: 'You spell it with an "i" not a "y".' And he was supposed to have bad eyesight.

PAT PARTRIDGE, League referee, in *Oh, Ref!*, **1979**.

An assassin. Brutal, badly intentioned and a bad sporstman.

OTTO GLORIA, Benfica manager, in *The European Cup 1955-80*.

There were times when Nobby should have drawn the wages of some of the people he played with. He not only did his job, he made sure everyone else did theirs.

HARRY GREGG, Manchester United team-mate 1960s, as above.

The players' player, *bête noire* of the purists, a tiny, toothless, urban, gesticulating figure, perennially in the bad books of referees and opponents. . .a player with no obvious physical or technical gifts, a poor passer of the ball, but a formidable marker and an extraordinary competitor.

BRIAN GLANVILLE, in *The History of the World Cup*, **1980**.

Gordon Strachan

He was playing much of the time from memory. But by God, what a memory.

RON ATKINSON, Manchester United manager, on Strachan's comeback after injury, **1985**.

Luis Suarez (Inter Milan)

A lovely fellow, great with our kids, as well as being an unbeliev-able player. He was like a gazelle, he would just float over the ground, and then bang – he would hit a thirty-yard ball into someone's path to open up the game.

GERRY HITCHENS, England centre-forward of early 1960s and team-mate of Suarez in Italy, in *The European Cup 1955-80*.

There were three famous midfield players, Sivori, Rivera and Suarez. Rivera I didn't rate as highly because I felt he could get a bit lost. Sivori had sensational skill, could beat you again and again, but had a terrible temper. He hated Herrera. For instance, I once saw him beat a man near the touchline, look up and drive the ball at Herrera on the bench. For me, Suarez was the best of the three.

GERRY HITCHENS, as above.

Brian Talbot

The country would be better off with more men like Brian Talbot, not only footballers, but train drivers, lorry drivers, everybody.

TERRY NEILL, Arsenal manager, **1979**.

Bert Trautmann

What manner of man is Trautmann? Certainly not one you would pass in a crowd. He is of the Nordic type, with blond hair, keen grey eyes, a gentle manner, a charming smile, and a deceptive air of indolence in response. But a steely look can come in those grey eyes; the thrust of a panther's spring into those clean, straight limbs; and few can pass with such lightning rapidity from complete immobility to energetic action. In straightforwardness and clean living he is a model for any young boy.

H. D. DAVIES on Manchester City's German goalkeeper in *Boy's Own Paper*, **1957**.

Bertie Vogts (W. Germany)

A team of eleven Bertie Vogtses would be unbeatable.

KEVIN KEEGAN, **1975**.

Ray Wilson

I don't think that I ever gave many fouls away. The most was when I played [for Huddersfield] against Stanley Matthews in his comeback game for Stoke City. I coughed twice and the referee blew.

RAY WILSON, former England full-back, in Martin Tyler, *Boys of '66*, **1981**.

Tony Woodcock

He's fast, strong, sharp and skilful but otherwise he's useless.

KEN BROWN, Norwich manager, **1982**.

Frank Worthington

The way he's losing his hair he'll be the first bald guy ever to do impressions of Elvis Presley.

GRAEME SOUNESS, **1984**.

Clubs

Arsenal 1920–30s

Only people who will not spend big money on transfer fees need apply.

ARSENAL advertisement in *Athletic News* for post of secretary-manager, **1925**. Herbert Chapman got the job.

Although I do not suggest that the Arsenal go on the defensive *even* for tactical purposes, I think it may be said that some of their best scoring chances have come when they have been driven back and then have broken away to strike suddenly and swiftly.

HERBERT CHAPMAN, Arsenal manager, **1930s**.

When I played for Arsenal, the saying there was, 'What we have, we hold.' That is, you start off with a point before you even run on to the field.

TED DRAKE, Arsenal and England centre-forward in *The Encyclopedia of Association Football*, **1960**.

At Highbury we went for results. Results meant getting goals so we cut the movements down from four passes to two. Our great ball was the long one and that opened the game up.

TED DRAKE, as above.

Where everybody made the mistake was to follow Arsenal in Chapman's day. At Highbury they needed fast-raiding wingers with an inside-forward hanging back, a defensive centre-half, and the use of the long pass. Everybody became imitators without having the right keys to the puzzle, and English football suffered in consequence. All of which was about as sensible as trying to whitewash the ceiling with green paint.

ARTHUR ROWE, as above.

It was the twentieth century, terse, exciting, spectacular, economic, devastating.

BERNARD JOY, journalist and England defender of 1930s, on Chapman's Arsenal.

Can it be believed that the Arsenal, in order to produce results, would cultivate a style that did not appeal to the crowd?

HERBERT CHAPMAN, **1930s**.

I well remember that as a boy, there was only one club for me – Arsenal.

PUSKAS in *Captain of Hungary*, **1955**.

You'll have to watch these Trojans. They don't play your game: they play an attacking game.

GEORGE ALLISON, Arsenal manager, acting himself doing pre-match talk in **1939** film, *The Arsenal Stadium Mystery*.

Arsenal Post-War

The place was like a palace. You were immediately conscious of belonging to something really big, really important. Everyone at Highbury lived, breathed, talked, ate and drank Arsenal. Everyone believed in the club; everyone was proud to be part of it. It was just like playing cricket for Yorkshire.

BRIAN CLOSE, England cricketer, on his spell with Arsenal (1950–51) in *I Don't Bruise Easily*, **1978**.

It seems ridiculous when I look at all that silverware, but also very wonderful. I believe that the present team is the greatest that has ever represented Arsenal.

DENIS HILL-WOOD, chairman, on **1971** 'double' team.

If he [Osvaldo Ardiles] had gone to Arsenal, they would have had him marking the opposing goalkeeper or something.

DANNY BLANCHFLOWER, **1981**.

Aston Villa 1960s

When I arrived at Aston Villa, by way of Portsmouth and Blackburn. . .it was like joining a Guards regiment after being with the RAOC. At first the atmosphere was overpowering. I was with a great club and it's not easy to live up to such greatness. At the same time I enjoyed the stimulus and the challenge. It wasn't until later, after I had left Villa, that I realized the peril of leaning too much on tradition. Villa were so mesmerized by past glories that they could not see what was happening to them until it was too late. Tradition was romanticized, a fatal mistake.

DEREK DOUGAN, in *Derek Dougan's Book of Soccer*, **1973**.

Blackburn Rovers 1880s

All hail, ye gallant Rover lads!
Etonians thought you were but cads:
They've found at football game their dads
By meeting Blackburn Rovers.

SONG before the **1882** FA Cup final. The Old Etonians won 1–0.

Bolton Wanderers 1950s

When I first came into the game, Bolton were the team everybody feared for their sheer brute force. Their England international full-back Tommy Banks used to say to Chelsea winger Peter Brabrook: 'If thou tries to get past me, lad, thou will get gravel rash. . . .' And a favourite comment from their rugged half-back Doug Hennin was: 'If my inside-forward 'appens to come through, chip him back to me. . .'

JIMMY GREAVES in *This One's On Me*, **1979**.

Brazil 1970

The Romanians were hard, but as far as I was concerned the Brazilians were harder; and if that seemed difficult to believe, I had the bruises and the soreness to prove my point. Jairzinho went right over the top of the ball and kicked my shins. . . .Pele had a go at me and I landed one back, so that was twice I had lost my temper which is unusual for me.

MARTIN PETERS at the Mexico World Cup, **1970**.

Bury 1900s

Their constant and consistent vanquishing of the dread bogie Poverty has been the most wonderful of all their performances.

PICKFORD and GIBSON, **1906**.

Celtic

His [Robert Kelly, the chairman] was the brain that fashioned the organization with Stein at its head. If he had a weakness it was his obsession with the players of the past and especially the great Celtic team of before the First World War. The accolade was put on the trip [to Lisbon] when he declared solemnly and it seemed with some pain, 'This was the greatest Celtic team of all time.' He might have expanded the adjective to Scottish or even British and nobody would have questioned his judgement.

JOHN RAFFERTY, *Scotsman* soccer correspondent, on the 1967 Lisbon Lions in *We'll Support You Evermore*, **1976**.

The thing I envy about Celtic and Rangers is the loyalty they get from their players. They're not interested in playing for anyone else.

HARRY CATTERICK, Everton manager, **1964**.

Charlton Athletic 1930s

Unmatched by the record of any club in the British Isles, cradle of Association Football, or Soccer, the history of Charlton Athletic, one of the most sensational aggregations of the booting game ever to essay an invasion of the United States and Canada, is truly monumental in athletic annals.

PROGRAMME NOTES, Illinois All Stars *v.* Charlton in Chicago, **1937**.

Chelsea

They have always played good football at Chelsea, but they have always played it across the field in the past, never through the field. They played the Scottish style of the past because they usually possessed a number of Scottish players, good players never getting anywhere.

TED DRAKE, Chelsea manager, in *The Encyclopedia of Association Football*, **1960**.

Chelsea are the most unusual of clubs. They have never done what every other club was doing at the same time as every other club was doing it.

RALPH FINN in *A History of Chelsea FC*, **1969**.

The Corinthians

The Corinthians of my day never trained, and I can safely say that the need of it was never felt. We were all fit and I think I could have played on for more than one and a half hours without being any the worse.

G. O. SMITH, centre-forward 1893–1901, in Edward Grayson, *Corinthians, Casuals and Cricketers*, **1955**.

I say, Bill, if there was to be a war, I'd sooner have the Corinthians than the Army on my side, wouldn't you?

SPECTATOR leaving the Oval after a vigorous match between an Army XI and the Corinthians in **1892–93**.

England 1966

People say England are a physical team. They have left out a word. They should say England are a physically fit team.

HAROLD SHEPHERDSON, trainer, on **1966** World Cup-winning team.

They canna play nane.

JIM BAXTER before England *v*. Scotland, **1967**. Scotland won 3–2.

England 1970

The English team had some outstanding players. Men like Banks, and Booby Moore, and Cooper and Bobby and Jack Charlton. They can play on any Brazilian team at any time – and that is no light compliment.

PELE after Brazil's victory over England, in *My Life and the Beautiful Game*, **1966**.

Estudiantes (1968 World Club champions)

We tried to find out everything possible about our rivals individually, their habits, their characters, their weaknesses and even about their private lives, so that we could goad them on the field, get them to react and risk being sent off.

JUAN RAMON VERON, Estudiantes player of 1968, talking in **1983**.

Hungary 1953–54

The Hungarians were just as great a team of pure footballers in the years 1936–39. . .as they were. . .when they beat us at Wembley. . . . But there was one vital difference. . .to the post-war Hungarian, to be a great footballer was a passport to a good living in a country where life wasn't very pleasant. Therefore their football became much more pungent, much more incisive, much more determined, much more ultimate in its performance. Where it was a performance of art and craft before, it was a performance again, but now with a goal – and I mean goal in both senses. Their finishing was meant. If they didn't finish, they famished.

ARTHUR ROWE in *The Encyclopedia of Association Football*, **1960**.

[They] have probably achieved at this point of time as great a mastery over a football as any team in history. By a perfect mixture of the short Continental game and the long pass English style they have found the best of both worlds, all this based upon quintessence of controlled speed and quick thinking. Their shooting, too, from all angles once more was deadly when it mattered.

GEOFFREY GREEN, journalist, on Hungary 7, England 1, Budapest **1954**.

The legend grew that Hungary played football on the carpet and used mainly short passes. . . . The actual figure of long passes was as many as ninety-four, most of them played in the first hour of the match. More than sixty were in the air. The general impression, too, was that Hungary's six goals were scored by means of clever movements which contained many short passes. Here again, the facts showed a different picture to the one which existed in the mind of the Press and the public. Only *one* of Hungary's goals came from a move which started in their half of the field.

STAN CULLIS, Wolves manager 1950s, in *All for the Wolves*, **1960**.

The 1954 Hungarian soccer masters did not go into the record books as the champions of the world. But they went into my personal memory file – and that of millions of other football-lovers – as the finest team ever to sort out successfully the intricacies of this wonderful game.

TOM FINNEY, Preston and England forward, in *Finney on Football*, **1958**.

Manchester United are like the Hungarian side of 1953 which set up little triangles of close passing all over the field and lured people up to it – and suddenly there would be a long pass, and some chap you hadn't been looking at would be streaking through to the England goal like lightning.

A. H. FABIAN, FA coach, schoolteacher and ex-Derby player, in *The Encyclopedia of Association Football*, **1960**.

Leeds United 1960s and 1970s

We had seven, eight, nine years of Leeds, and that was too much. They played foul football, and showed that you could get away with cheating. So players come in with kicks and bruises all over them, and get their pay packets and think, 'No win bonus again; perhaps it's time we started this lark.'

ARTHUR ROWE in *Foul! Book of Football*, **1975**.

What a terrible team to play against. A pain. You try and take a throw-in. They have got everybody picked up, a man in front of the winger and a man on you. You can't even take a throw-in. It demoralizes you. Leeds have developed that into an art. Nobody outside the game knows what it is like. It is like some fellow running up to your desk or work bench all day and sticking a pin in you then running away. The cumulative effect is drastic.

EAMON DUNPHY in *Only a Game?*, **1976**.

I didn't used to be frightened on the football pitch. But I was always relieved to get off in one piece, particularly during those mid and late 1960s when the likes of Leeds United were kicking anything that moved.

JIMMY GREAVES in *This One's On Me*, **1979**.

Leeds should have been instantly relegated after being branded one of the dirtiest clubs in Britain. I feel strongly that the two pence-ha'penny suspended fine is the most misguided piece of woolly thinking ever perpetrated by the FA, a body hardly noted for its commonsense. It's like breathalysing a drunken driver, getting a positive reading, giving him his keys back and telling him to watch it on the way home.

BRIAN CLOUGH, August **1973** – a year before he became Leeds manager.

I watched the so-called analysis of the new Leeds on Match of the Day, and to be honest it was the best laugh I've had in ages. I kept visualizing their players helping old ladies across the street and kissing babies in prams.

MALCOLM MACDONALD, **1973**.

Looking back over the outstanding club sides in England over the past thirty years, I suppose Leeds have to be ranked alongside the Manchester United side that was partially destroyed at Munich, the United side of the late Sixties which boasted Best, Law and Charlton, the Liverpool side of the Seventies, the Arsenal double-winning side, and the Spurs side of the early Sixties.

BOBBY ROBSON, in *Time on the Grass*, **1982**.

If I try something a bit saucy the Dutch and the Belgians I play with shout 'Hard luck' or 'Try again' when it doesn't come off. At Leeds when that happened I'd turn round and there'd be someone with his fist up, threatening to chin me. One of my own team-mates!

DUNCAN McKENZIE on playing for Anderlecht after Leeds, **1976**.

I don't think I'll become a manager when my playing days are over. . . . I would rather teach 15–18 year-olds and make sure they're brought up with good disciplines and habits – the kind of grounding, in fact, that I had myself at Leeds United.

NORMAN HUNTER, Bristol City and former England defender, **1978**.

Liverpool

Liverpool are the most uncomplicated side in the world. They all drive forward when they've got the ball, and they all get behind it when they haven't.

JOE MERCER, **1973**.

The team of our time, the ideal model of the contemporary team in which collective qualities have risen above individual qualities, as outstanding as such famous clubs as Real Madrid and Ajax.

MILJAN MILJANIC, Yugoslavia manager.

They are admired from Buenos Aires to Belgrade, and have given many clubs an inferiority complex.

MILJAN MILJANIC.

We do things together. I'd walk into the toughest dockside pub in the world with this lot. Because you know that if things got tough, nobody would 'bottle' it, and scoot off.

EMLYN HUGHES on his Liverpool colleagues in 1976–77, in Brian James, *Journey to Wembley*, **1977**.

It was one of Bill Shankly's ideas. A bit of psychology. Playing here lifts good pros, puts the bad 'uns under pressure. We counted. . .there were more bad pros about than good 'uns. So the sign went up.

BOB PAISLEY explaining the 'This is Anfield' plaque over the players tunnel. Brian James, *Journey to Wembley*, **1977**.

I told you we'd found the right ground, boss!

MALCOLM MACDONALD pointing out the plaque to Newcastle manager Joe Harvey.

It's daft, I know, but if we win the next dozen games 1–0 we will end up as the greatest British team ever.

JOHN TOSHACK as Liverpool's chase for the treble approached its climax in 1976–77. Brian James, *Journey to Wembley*, **1977**.

There are two great teams on Merseyside. Liverpool and Liverpool Reserves.

BILL SHANKLY.

Mind, I've been here during the bad times too. One year we came second.

BOB PAISLEY, **1979**.

A lot of teams beat us, do a lap of honour and don't stop running. They live too long on one good result. I remember Jimmy Adamson crowing after Burnley had beaten us once that his players were in a different league. At the end of the season they were.

BOB PAISLEY, **1979**.

I felt like General Custer with one bullet left.

BILLY ASHCROFT, Middlesbrough defender, after 4–0 defeat by Liverpool, **1979**.

Our only chance would have been to sandbag the eighteen-yard line and pick them off one by one with rifles.

MICHAEL ROBINSON, Manchester City striker, after 4–0 defeat by Liverpool, whom he later joined, **1979**.

I went to Leeds because I thought I might win some honours at last. We can't all play for bloody Liverpool, can we?

TONY CURRIE, Leeds and England midfield player, **1980**.

By our standards we didn't deserve to win it this year. But by everybody else's, we did.

GRAEME SOUNESS on Liverpool's third consecutive League championship, **1983–4**.

It was not the Liverpool we are used to seeing. I don't know what they were trying to do, and I don't think they knew either.

KEVIN RATCLIFFE, Everton captain, in February **1986**. Three months later Liverpool had done the double.

Manchester United 'The Babes'

In all modesty, my summing-up of 1955–56 and 1956–57 must be that no club in the country could live with Manchester United.

MATT BUSBY in *My Story*, **1957**.

United will go on
The road back may be long and hard but with the memory of those who died at Munich, of their stirring achievements and wonderful sportsmanship ever with us, Manchester United will rise again.

H. P. HARDMAN, United chairman, United *v*. Nottingham Forest programme, **1958**.

I may be thought odd, but when I think of Manchester United, I think of Roger Byrne, Duncan Edwards and Eddie Colman before the crash, and of Harry Gregg, Bill Foulkes and Nobby Stiles afterwards. Best, Law and Crerand were replaceable somehow. They weren't the heart of the team.

BOBBY CHARLTON.

If you went through the Manchester team which won the League in 1957, for instance, you would have to look very hard to find your truly great players. Look at the whole forward line – Berry, Whelan, Taylor, Viollet, Pegg – and you will search very hard to find a really outstanding player. . . .But because they were playing to order and precision, with method and movement; because they were fluid and not trying to do what they could not do (which is the downfall of so many people); because they were doing things within their limits, they were successful.

ARTHUR ROWE in *The Encyclopedia of Association Football*, **1960**.

Others might fight their way out of trouble with flailing boot, but surely not United. Other clubs might have little faith in football as a contest of skill, an expression of personality, but United surely would live or die with style. When the pressure came they behaved just like another club in trouble.

TONY PAWSON, journalist and former Charlton player, on United's response to the threat of relegation in the early 1970s in *The Football Managers*, **1973**.

Moscow Dynamo 1945

I count myself fortunate to have seen Moscow Dynamo twice during their short tour of Britain. Especially fortunate in seeing their brilliant display in the opening match against Chelsea. It was about the finest exhibition I have seen in Britain since the Corinthians were a great side; classic combination and teamwork; superb ball control – the true Cornthian style, now called the Scottish style.

SIR GODFREY INCE, captain of London University team to Moscow in **1914**.

The speed of the Russian players and the brilliance of their foot-ball showed just how far our players had gone back during the war, but this Moscow Dynamo team was a club in name only. The players had been specially assembled from four towns, were the pick of the players from the whole of Russia, and had been drilled into a brilliant machine sent to this country on a political mission with orders that they must not fail.

TOM WHITTAKER, former Arsenal manager, in *Tom Whittaker's Arsenal Story*, **1958**.

Queen's Park 1870–80s

Surely the greatest of all clubs! I have a great admiration, a great respect, a great esteem – nay, even a great affection for the Queen's Park club. What pigmies some of our strictly modern clubs seem, how thin and poor their records, when a comparison is instituted between them and Queen's Park! What a halo of romance and glory surrounds the Queen's Park club! What a wealth of honourable tradition is theirs!

WILLIAM McGREGOR, founder of the Football League, in Pickford and Gibson, **1906**.

Rangers

All that running we did. No wonder they encouraged the big men. The dressing room was built for them – we used to laugh because little Willie Henderson had to jump up to reach his peg. When I was there the defenders were men like Bobby Shearer, who was built like a tree trunk.

WILLIE STEVENSON, Rangers and Liverpool wing-half in the 1950s and 1960s, in Motson and Rowlinson, *The European Cup 1955–80*, **1980**.

Rangers like the big, strong, powerful fellows, with a bit of strength and solidity in the tackle rather than the frivolous, quick-moving stylists like Jimmy Johnstone, small, tiptoe-through-the-tulips type of players who excite the people.

WILLIE WADDELL, manager, **1972**.

Real Madrid 1955–60

There was no doubt that they were a good side, but they could be a bit naughty at times, and that includes di Stefano.

JOHN BERRY, Manchester United winger.

To be honest I was terribly pleased I wasn't playing. I saw di Stefano and these others, and I thought these people just aren't human. It's not the sort of game I've been taught.

BOBBY CHARLTON on watching Real Madrid v. Manchester United European Cup semi-final, **1957**.

The best I ever saw, apart from Brazil.

JUST FONTAINE, Reims and France centre-forward.

We never had a blackboard, and hardly ever talked about our opponents, and this attitude helped us to turn games our way. In the days of di Stefano we just came to the stadium, put on our shirts and played.

FRANCISCO GENTO, Real winger.

They could dish out the hard stuff too, especially Santamaria. People gloat about them and say they never kicked anybody. Well, they certainly kicked me.

JOHN CHARLES, Juventus centre-forward.

Stevenson, refusing to believe a team which had put twelve goals past his side [Rangers] could possibly lose, immediately put £5 on Eintracht to beat Real at Hampden.

MOTSON and ROWLINSON *The European Cup 1955–80*. Real won 7–3 in the final.

In half a year I earned more money with Real Madrid than in my whole professional career.

MIGUEL TORRES on his loan period from Real Zaragoza, **1957**.

Scotland 1928 'The Wembley Wizards'

Jimmy McMullan, captain of the Wembley Wizards team, was asked by a sportswriter after that memorable match if there had been a plan to beat England. Jimmy grinned, and said: 'Aye, we laid down a plan. It was a simple one but a stern one. I told the boys: "Now I don't want any unnecessary talking. Get on with the game and don't talk to opponents or the referee." ' The awed reporter said: 'That was good. Certainly it worked.' McMullan replied: 'Did it heck! Alex James's tongue went like a gramophone from the kick-off.' The reporter asked: 'Did you tick him off?' 'Don't be daft,' said Jimmy. 'How could I? If his tongue went like a gramophone, so did his feet.'

HUGH TAYLOR on Scotland's 5–1 win over England at Wembley, 1928, in *Great Masters of Scottish Football*, **1968**.

Tottenham Hotspur 1900s

Than the famous Spurs there is probably no more popular club in England. Did they not recover the Association Cup for the south? Did they not play pretty and effective football? Are they not scrupulously fair? Are they not perfectly managed?

PICKFORD and GIBSON, **1906**.

Tottenham Hotspur 1950–52

The great thing we built on basically was accuracy. We had two or three great performers, and we had a lot who were not. But they were all made to look great players because of the system we adopted, and because they played in a winning side.

ARTHUR ROWE in *The Encyclopedia of Association Football*, **1960**.

Tottenham Hotspur 'double' side 1960–61

They've become lazy. Our play means a lot of hard work, and our forwards in particular have not been keen to carry on that hard work. There has been a lack of desire for action.

BILL NICHOLSON after Spurs had picked up only one point from three games. The next match was won 5–0. Julian Holland, *Spurs – the Double*, **1961**.

Watford 1980s

Watford are setting English football back ten years.

TERRY VENABLES, **1982**.

How obtuse. If Watford could put the game back ten years, it would be in a better state than it is now. There would be no £1 million players and wages to suit, there would be less debts, and more fans would be watching.

DANNY BLANCHFLOWER, **1982**.

Imagine Franz Beckenbauer trying to play for Watford. He'd just be in the way.

FRANK McLINTOCK, **1982**.

West Ham United

To be sure they had some of the aristocrat's qualities: indolence and unwillingness to sweat, a reluctance to soil their hands. In a way they were con-men. Like all good con-artists they had a certain style. Their play had a smooth, slick quality; it was seductive. Aficionados often purred at the sight of the Hammers and denounced football for denying the game's prizes to the purists they saw in West Ham. It was true they had talent but so did Leeds and Liverpool. They are the real contenders, the true aristocrats. What West Ham lack are values. When the challenge came, their lack of integrity left them at the mercy of the better prepared, the people who worked at the game.

EAMON DUNPHY, in *Only a Game?*, **1976**.

One of the first teams to adopt the new negative style were West Ham United, but it failed to bring them success. From 1966 onwards, despite having England's Moore, Hurst and Peters in their side, they became a team who were always fighting for survival rather than one trying to win something.

DENIS LAW, an opponent with Manchester United in *An Autobiography*, **1979**.

You can forget the purist stuff now. We've finished with that. When people start to compare us with West Ham, that's when we'll start to worry.

PETER TAYLOR, assistant manager of Derby County, **1973**.

The crowds at West Ham haven't been rewarded by results, but they keep turning up because of the good football they see. Other clubs will suffer from the old bugbear that results count more than anything. This has been the ruination of English soccer.

RON GREENWOOD after England's failure to qualify for World Cup finals in **1977**.

I'm fed up with being a good-looking loser. Had too much of it at West Ham. How many times did we have to slink away from little grounds, while the home lot were trying not to laugh out loud?

GEOFF HURST in Brian James, *Journey to Wembley*, **1977**.

TREVOR BROOKING: It looks as though your side is a bit younger these days?
JOHN LYALL: No, it's just that now we all tackle.

EXCHANGE between the radio commentator and his former manager, **1986**.

Wimbledon 1986

At this club if we go to a game we don't usually have a full meal on the way home, just a snack. The players have to wash their own kit, provide their own towels for training and have to clean their own boots.

DAVE BASSETT, manager of the side who won promotion to the First Division nine years after leaving the Southern League.

They've mucked up my weekend, so now I'm going to muck up theirs.

DAVE BASSETT, calling his players in for training on Sunday after Cup defeat by Millwall.

Wolverhampton Wanderers 1950s

On the morning of the match, Stan Cullis sent for me and two of the other apprentices, and told us to go out and water the pitch. We thought he was out of his mind. It was December and it had been raining incessantly for four days. When I watched the match in the evening, I understood what he was up to. The Hungarians were two up in fifteen minutes and playing superbly. It was the best football I have ever seen, brilliant first-time movement. But the pitch was getting heavier and heavier. The mud just wore the Hungarians out.

RON ATKINSON, later to become Manchester United manager, on Wolves 3, Honved 2, 1954. Motson and Rowlinson, *The European Cup 1955–80*, **1980**.

Hail, Wolves 'Champions of the World' now

Daily Mail headline.

We must wait for Wolves to visit Budapest and Moscow before we proclaim their invincibility. And there are other clubs of international prowess, like Milan and Real Madrid.

GABRIEL HANOT, French journalist and founder of the European Cup, in *L'Equipe*.

We won it [the League] in 1954 and again four years later, by playing attacking football, which was my whole philosophy. In the late 1950s we scored more than 100 goals for three or four years in succession. Of course that made us more vulnerable at the back, but that was our style. To win the European Cup required a different style. It required players to go against their natural game, and this I was not prepared to do.

STAN CULLIS, Wolves manager 1950s, in *The European Cup 1955–80*, **1980**.

I don't fancy Wolves to win the European Cup. Their power football may get them through another round, but I cannot see them winning the trophy.

DENNIS VIOLLET, Manchester United and England player, in a newspaper article before European Cup quarter-final, Barcelona *v.* Wolves in **1960**. Barcelona won 4–0 and 5–2; Viollet was reprimanded by the Football League.

One well-known manager from a Midlands club said in the board-room afterwards, 'Football! That wasn't football. Two of the goals came from long belts down the field by the goalkeeper. They never sign a goalkeeper unless he can kick eighty yards.'

STAN CULLIS on Wolves' 1957 victory over Real Madrid, in *All for the Wolves*, **1960**.

Wolves' success does Mr Cullis great credit, but it has also done much damage to the game in general in England because so many lesser managers have attempted to ape the Wolves-Cullis technique. Artistry with the ball is not all-important with Wolverhampton Wanderers.

JIMMY McILROY, Burnley and Northern Ireland midfield player, in *Right Inside Soccer*, **1960**.

Wolverhampton in my opinion give the ball a little bit too much wallop down the middle and tell the centre-forward to go. They are inclined to belt the ball. It was their two fast-raiding wingers, Mullen and Hancocks, which led to their success for some years with a long ball from wing to wing and through the middle.

TED DRAKE, Chelsea manager, in *The Encyclopedia of Association Football*, **1960**.

Wolverhampton Wanderers 1980s

I told them 'I'm glad I didn't have you four defending me when I had my court case. The judge would've put his black cap on.'

TOMMY DOCHERTY, manager on Wolves' defence, **1984**.

It's a bit like joining the Titanic in mid-voyage.

RACHEL HEYHOE-FLINT on joining Wolves as public relations officer, **1985**.

I just opened the trophy cabinet. Two Japanese prisoners of war came out.

TOMMY DOCHERTY, **1985**.

Our strikers couldn't score in a brothel.

DOCHERTY after his team had scored 5 goals in 19 games during the second of three successive relegation seasons, **1985**.

I tried to sign one of the Vietnamese boat people last week, and he said, 'Mr Docherty, I'd love to join Wolves, but I've left one sinking ship already.'

TOMMY DOCHERTY.

We don't use a stop-watch to judge our golden goal competition now. We use a calendar.

DOCHERTY on Wolves' goal famine, **1985**.

Wolves couldn't afford our tea-lady, let alone Cyrille Regis.

JOHN POYNTON, Coventry chairman, on Docherty's claim that he tried to sign Regis, **1985**.

How can you work for people you never see? Howard Hughes could be more easily found than the people who run Wolves.

TOMMY DOCHERTY after being sacked by the Bhatti brothers, **1985**.

I just happen to believe in this club, like Eddie Clamp's mother, who's still doing the club's laundry after 30 years.

BILL McGARRY on succeeding the Doc, **1985**. He resigned after 61 days.

There's basically no difference between the Wolves you see now and the Wolves who enjoyed the heady days of the Fifties. They just happen to be in the Third Division.

GORDON DIMBLEBY, Wolves chief executive, **1985**.

2

Of Managers and Coaches

Life and Work

All managers are frustrated players.

JOE MERCER, who managed numerous clubs in **1950/70s**.

The manager's job in those days was to assemble a good team. Once he had done that he just let them go out and play. There was none of this blackboard nonsense you hear about today. Team talk? Johnny [Cochrane, the manager] used to stick his head around the dressing-room door just before a match, smoking a cigar and smelling of whisky, and ask, 'Who are we playing today?' We'd reply, 'Arsenal, boss,' and he'd just say, 'Oh well, we'll piss that lot,' before shutting the door and leaving us to it.

RAICH CARTER, on playing for Sunderland in the **1930s**.

Don't try to keep your job by taking advice on football from the Chairman. Do what he says and you will lose it soon enough on your results.

HARRY STORER, Coventry, Birmingham, Derby manager and mentor to Clough and Taylor.

[A manager] is there to be seen and exposed to his players. They will know him within seven days. They will sort out his strengths and weaknesses immediately.

EAMON DUNPHY in *Only a Game?*, **1976**.

> Reserving at your will
> The promise of my skills
> Shining stars treated with such
> contempt

JOHN FARMER, former Stoke goalkeeper, on managers' treatment of players, from his poem 'Upon the Shelf'.

Managers in the Third and Fourth Divisions have chips on their shoulders because they think they should be in better jobs. They go about whingeing all day.

JIMMY GREAVES, **1984**.

I thought he'd gone back on the drink.

JOHN McGOVERN, Bolton manager, replying to Greaves.

Great teams don't need managers. Brazil won the World Cup (in 1970) playing exhilarating football, with a manager they'd had for three weeks. Now what influence can a man have who's only been with them for that length of time? What about Real Madrid at their greatest? You can't even remember who the manager was.

DANNY BLANCHFLOWER, **1972**.

A manager's aggravation is self-made. All a manager has to do is keep eleven players happy – the eleven in the reserves. The first team are happy because they are in the first team.

RODNEY MARSH, **1972**.

Lots of times managers have to be cheats and conmen. We are the biggest hypocrites. We cheat. The only way to survive is by cheating.

TOMMY DOCHERTY, **1979**.

Most managers come into the game intending to be honest, but too many of them discover that life becomes a little easier if they start bending the rules. Some try to bend the rules all of the time, and I suspect that very nearly all try some of the time. Indeed, I think there are some qualities common to almost every manager who has not only made it to the top but managed to stay there. This small and special breed are, very nearly to a man, devious and ruthless and selfish.

ALAN HARDAKER, secretary of the Football League, in *Hardaker of the League*, **1977**.

Look son, imagine this is a huge pot of money. Franny's had a bit, Colin's dipped in, of course Malcolm's had a dollop, in fact all the lads have had a bit. . .so there's none left for you.

JOE MERCER to City player seeking raise, in *Another Breath of Fred Eyre*, **1982**.

Yes, I thought the secretary did very well. He booked us into some very nice hotels.

MALCOLM ALLISON on being informed that he and the Manchester City secretary were to receive the same bonus for the team's promotion to Division I.

I'm not just the manager – to save money I'm trainer, coach and physio too, though I have a bloke who does the sponge for me on Saturdays.

PETER MADDEN on life with Rochdale, **1981**.

The sign was up – 'No hawkers. No circulars. No coaches.'

GEORGE RAYNOR, later Sweden's World Cup manager, on trying to get a job in England in the **1940s**.

I asked the manager for a ball to train with. He couldn't have looked more horrified if I'd asked for a transfer. He told me they never used a ball at Barnsley. The theory was that we'd be hungry for it on Saturday if we didn't see it for the rest of the week. I told him that, come Saturday, I probably wouldn't recognize it.

DANNY BLANCHFLOWER on his first English club.

Planned coaching, like any other form of control, gets into a bureaucratic state which not only continues its mistakes, but tends to increase them.

BILLY WALKER, Nottingham Forest manager in 1950s, in Tony Pawson, *The Football Managers*, **1973**.

They are all well-spoken, they are all good-living, and all in their different ways deferential to authority.

BILLY WALKER on coaches (as above).

•

I am grateful to my father for all the coaching he did *not* give me.

FERENC PUSKAS, **1961**.

If one day the tacticians reached perfection, the result would be a 0–0 draw – and there'd be nobody there to see it.

PAT CRERAND, Manchester United and Scotland midfield player, **1970**.

You need an 'O' level or a degree to understand the tactics at Old Trafford.

GORDON HILL, Manchester United winger, on his transfer to Derby, **1978**.

Recently my coach underwent a course on Attacking Football run by the FA. He didn't see a goal scored during the whole week.

ALEC STOCK, Fulham manager, **1973**.

Everywhere I go there are coaches. Schoolmasters telling young boys not to do this and not to do that and generally scaring the life out of the poor little devils. Junior clubs playing with sweepers, one and a half men up front, no wingers, four across the middle. They are frightened to death of losing, even at their tender age, and it makes me cry.

ALEC STOCK in *A Little Thing Called Pride*, **1982**.

I'm uncoachable, it's true. That's because I know more than the stupid coaches.

GIORGIO CHINAGLIA, New York Cosmos player, **1979**.

Some of the jargon is frightening. They talk of 'getting round the back' and sound like burglars. They say 'You've got to make more positive runs' or 'You're too negative'. That sounds as though you're filling the team with electricians. But people talk like this without real depth or knowledge of what they're really talking about.

BOB PAISLEY, **1980**.

We were getting a certain type of manager coming into the game. They were being turned out like Ford Fiestas. They produced a couple of coaching badges and called themselves managers.

BRIAN CLOUGH in tribute to Bob Paisley, **1983**.

I sat in my car one day, first in line when the lights changed. I stopped and instinctively everyone behind stopped in sequence. I realized that football was that simple. My team played a marvellous eight-man move last week and one of the kids shouted 'Traffic Lights'. I could have kissed him.

ALAN BALL, Portsmouth youth coach, **1983**.

When I arrived in the summer, one of my predecessors told the Spanish press that Meester Terry would be gone by Christmas, but he forgot to say which year.

TERRY VENABLES, Barcelona manager, **1984**.

I will never tolerate slackness. If it enters a team there can be no success that is worthwhile. That, at any rate, is my view, and frankly I cannot be bothered with any man unless he is prepared to give his whole mind to the job.

HERBERT CHAPMAN, Arsenal manager, **1930s**.

Age does not count. It's what you know about football that matters. I know I am better than the 500 or so managers who have been sacked since the war. If they had known anything about the game, they wouldn't have lost their jobs.

BRIAN CLOUGH, on becoming Hartlepools United manager in 1965.

In this business, you've got to be a dictator or you haven't got a chance.

BRIAN CLOUGH, 1965.

If you threaten certain spiv players, you must carry it out and not let them get away with it. A football team only has eleven players. It just needs one bad 'un to affect the rest. In ICI, with thousands and thousands of people, you can afford to carry scoundrels. Not in a football team.

BRIAN CLOUGH, 1973.

There has been less respect from the players, and no manager can work without that.

BILL NICHOLSON on resigning as Spurs manager, 1974.

I tried to help the younger players, to be friendly and to respond to their demands. But I must have looked and sound like an old man to them. Sometimes when I got home at the end of the day, I'd think 'Jesus Christ! What am I trying to do? These players are entitled to their own values, but why should I have to change mine?'

DANNY BLANCHFLOWER, on his spell as Chelsea manager in the 1970s.

The image of football has to be vastly improved, its behaviour as well as its attacking outlook. I was responsible for things that were not right at Leeds, but now I've got the job of improving the game at all levels. As players you don't realize how bad the dissent and the snarling looks in close-up on TV.

DON REVIE addressing eighty selected players in Manchester after his appointment as England manager, 1974.

Loyalty and respect seem old-fashioned words nowadays, but, as far as professional football is concerned, these are still the most important qualities of all in my view.

DON REVIE as England manager in **1975** – two years before leaving the job for Dubai – in *FA Book of Soccer*.

Behind Sophia Loren, but only because she has a better figure.

HELENIO HERRERA, Inter Milan coach, in **1965** replying to question, 'What would be your position in an Italian popularity poll?'

It's easy to do it at home to York, but can they do it at Mansfield next week when there are coal-heaps all over the place and it's pissing down with rain?

IAN BRANFOOT, Reading manager, after victory over Fourth Division leaders York, **1984**.

Gimmick is a word used by jealous people to describe an idea they wish they'd thought of first.

JIMMY HILL, Coventry manager, on the club's 'Sky Blue Revolution' in the **1960s**.

Whichever teams win the Championship in the next twenty years, and I hope teams like Rochdale and Halifax will be amongst them, none of them will have as hard a job as we had. We did it with twelve players. Those London bums can't explain it.

BRIAN CLOUGH on Derby's title-win, **1972**.

Success? Tell me that date when my obituary is going to appear and I'll tell you whether I've been a success or not. If I get to sixty I shall have done pretty well.

BRIAN CLOUGH, **1973**.

A em not an electrician.

SIR ALF RAMSEY to television commentator Hugh Johns who had asked him when floodlights might come back on, World Cup **1974**.

I'm not being sacked and I'm not going to resign. There is no panic in the camp. These rumours seem to have started because we are not quite the glamour team we used to be. Maybe we are not, but you cannot stay on top all the time and we have had a longer run than usual.

MATT BUSBY in article headed 'I'm Not Getting the Sack', in *All Football* (*Inc. Greyhound Outlook & Sports Pictures*), **1951**.

If the manager keeps saying, 'We'll win it, we'll win it, we'll win it,' eventually they believe you.

ALLY MacLEOD, Scotland manager, before **1978** World Cup.

No one will ever equal Sir Matt Busby's achievements and influence at Old Trafford, but I'd like to go down as someone who did nearly as much. . . .I'll be happy if at the end of the day people say, 'Well, there could only be one Sir Matt but T.D. came close to his standards and was the right man to follow on.'

TOMMY DOCHERTY, **1974**.

I have been punished for falling in love. What I have done has nothing at all to do with my track record as a manager.

DOCHERTY on his sacking by Manchester United in **1977** for 'breach of contract' after admitting an affair with the wife of the club physio.

I stood up and was counted.

ROGER HYND on being sacked as Motherwell manager, **1978**.

The Year of the Hamstring.

RON ATKINSON, Manchester United manager, reeling from injury blows, **1985**.

Of course I'd like to entertain as we did for four years in the Second Division – but we are boxing against a different class of opposition now.

IAN GREAVES, Bolton manager, **1979**.

Dunfermline Athletic had been my whole life, but there is one sure way to disassociate yourself from a football club – and that is by becoming its manager.

ANDY DICKSON on being sacked as Dunfermline manager, **1960**. In Jim Paterson and Douglas Scott, *Black and White Magic*.

I took over on a caretaker basis initially. They wanted to see if I was any good. But I'm permanent now – as long as we're winning.

MICK BUXTON, Huddersfield Town manager, **1979**.

Like Brian Clough I find it impossible to keep my mouth shut.

JOHN BOND, Norwich manager, **1979**.

It's easy enough to get to Ireland. Just a straight walk across the Irish sea as far as I'm concerned.

BRIAN CLOUGH, confirming his application for the Republic's manager's job, **1985**.

There are only two certainties in this life. People die, and football managers get the sack.

EOIN HAND, Limerick and Republic of Ireland manager, **1980**.

They offered me a handshake of £10,000 to settle amicably. I told them they would have to be more amicable than that.

TOMMY DOCHERTY on losing Preston job, **1981**.

There's no excitement. Tommy's just been sacked again, that's all.

MARY BROWN, Docherty's companion, to doorstepping pressmen.

You're welcome to my home phone number, gentlemen. But please remember not to ring me during 'The Sweeney'.

RON ATKINSON, to the press on his appointment as Manchester United manager, **1981**.

I don't drink, I don't smoke, and I'm getting fed up with gardening. I've no interests at all apart from football and family.

GORDON LEE on being out of work after dismissal from Everton manager's job, **1981**.

It's bloody tough being a legend.

RON ATKINSON, **1983**.

When I said even my Missus could save Derby from relegation, I was exaggerating.

PETER TAYLOR, **1982**.

With about two minutes to go I looked across at their bench, and I thought, 'When the whistle goes, I'm going to go across there, shake hands and say "All the best," and then when they've gone in I'm going to go mad.'

ALAN BUCKLEY, Walsall manager, after Milk Cup win at Arsenal, **1983**.

Nicholas's frustration doesn't bother me. I'm worried about my frustration. At least he gets a kick of the ball, once in a while.

TERRY NEILL, Arsenal manager, on the settling-in problems of his new signing, Charlie Nicholas, in **1983**. Neill was sacked a month later.

I've not learned too much about football, but I've become an expert in company law.

LENNIE LAWRENCE, Charlton manager on club's financial crisis, **1984**.

I've appointed Maurice Setters as my assistant. He's well placed living in Doncaster.

JACK CHARLTON after taking the Republic of Ireland manager's job, **1986**.

I think I have the best job in the country.

BOBBY ROBSON, England manager, **1985**.

Brazilians are too expensive and the French are not available.

EGYPTIAN FA SPOKESMAN, on criticism of the appointment of Mike Smith, former Wales manager, as national coach, **1985**.

It was a Limpalong Leslie sort of match.

PETER SHREEVE, Spurs manager, after 4–2 win *v.* Coventry, **1985**.

It was a bad day at Black Rock.

SHREEVE after 5–1 defeat by Watford a fortnight later, **1985**.

What's the bottom line in adjectives?

SHREEVE after home defeat by Coventry, **1986**.

Albion wear a "No Smoking" sign on their shirts. How the hell could I go there when I'm still fagging it like a maniac?

IAN GREAVES, Mansfield manager, on turning down the West Brom job, **1985**.

REPORTER: What's the Gidman situation, Ron? Is he in plaster?
RON ATKINSON: No, he's in Marbella.

EXCHANGE after West Brom *v.* United game, **1985**.

It's difficult to pull your socks up when you haven't got any socks to pull up.

JOHN BOND, Swansea manager, on club's financial plight, **1985**.

The Boss

Ron Atkinson

As far as he's concerned, he is God. There's nobody big enough to tell him what to do.

MARGARET ATKINSON, wife of Manchester United manager, after news broke of his extra-marital affair, **1984**.

This person suffers from erotic fantasies. He thinks a lot about sex, though he is very devoted to his mother.

GRAPHOLOGIST analysing Atkinson's writing, on ITV's FA Cup final coverage, **1985**.

It's rumoured that Man United are trying to sign Michel Platini, just in case they get a free-kick on the edge of the box this season. . . .

WHEN SATURDAY COMES fanzine – in the wake of Atkinson's heavy buying for United, **1986**.

The Manchester United manager. . .what's his name? You know, the Tank.

ROBERT MAXWELL, Oxford chairman, **1984**.

Tony Book

When the nuclear holocaust comes, I only hope I'm standing next to Booky.

MANCHESTER CITY PLAYER on Book's survival powers at Maine Road.

I wish Tony Book all that he wished me when I was in the manager's chair.

RON SAUNDERS after Book replaced him as Manchester City manager, **1974**.

Sir Matt Busby

Matt Busby is a symbol of everything that is best in our great national game.

SIR HAROLD WILSON.

He does not hand out toffees when he calls you into his office.

NOBBY STILES.

Father of Football.

BOOK TITLE by David Miller.

When Matt and Stan Cullis were first building their sides some of us who had been around before the war said to them, 'You're crazy. The young players today aren't any good, you're wasting your time.' But he knew what he was about.

JOE MERCER.

The great thing about Busby was that you would go in there fighting and full of demands. And he would give you nothing at all. He might even take a tenner off your wages. And you would come out thinking 'What a great guy.' I remember going in there once, absolutely livid. And ten minutes later I came out, no better off, walking on air. Delighted.

EAMON DUNPHY in *Only a Game?*, **1976**.

Herbert Chapman

Herbert Chapman worked himself to death for Arsenal, and if that is going to be my fate too, then I'll accept it.

TOM WHITTAKER, Arsenal manager, before his death in **1956**.

Never have I seen Herbert Chapman look so miserably unhappy. . .The team which he had made one of the greatest in the history of football, beaten by a fifth-rate side. Napoleon must have felt like that in Russia, 121 years before.

CLIFF BASTIN, Arsenal winger, on Arsenal's FA Cup calamity at Walsall, **1933**, in *Cliff Bastin Remembers*.

He was not a blustering bully. Chapman, who gave few words of praise and fewer of blame, inspired awe and respect, rather than fear. He had complete command of us all.

CLIFF BASTIN.

In the old days when Herbert Chapman reigned as the daddy of them all, a manager's job was worthwhile, because Chapman and many of his contemporaries really were managers in *sole* charge of the club. Directors dared not interfere or criticize Chapman, and players like myself would never attempt to carry on like some of the stars do today. Imagine a footballer telling Herbert Chapman he wouldn't sign for Arsenal until his wife had seen the house!

JIMMY SEED, ex-Spurs and England player, and Charlton Athletic manager, in *The Jimmy Seed Story*, **1958**.

Brian Clough

He is a kind of Rolls Royce Communist.

MALCOLM ALLISON, **1973**.

He has criticized Sir Matt Busby, me personally, Norman Hunter, Peter Lorimer, Billy Bremner, Peter Storey. . .people whose records stand to be seen. He talks about honesty. If honesty is going to destroy the game, you are doing it a great disservice.

DON REVIE, **1974**.

He's the best manager in the game. He's never been a failure. So why should he start here? Why should he start with me?

JUSTIN FASHANU three days after the Nottingham Forest manager had suspended him and told him he had no future with the club, **1982**.

Clough talks in riddles. He says things like, 'If you were half as flamboyant on the pitch as you are off it, you'd be a world-beater.' What good is that?

JUSTIN FASHANU, **1982**.

I was wrong to sign for Mr Clough. I'd heard of his reputation – but I just don't understand him. We rarely see the manager during the week but we can find him in the papers every day.

FRANS THIJSSEN, Nottingham Forest player, **1983**.

A player can never feel too sure of himself with Clough. That's his secret.

ARCHIE GEMMILL, Nottingham Forest midfield player, in Peter Taylor, *With Clough by Taylor*, **1980**.

Kenny Dalglish

He'll probably make a better manager than many of those about. He loves football. I see those blokes like Malcolm Allison and Terry Neill trying to fool everyone by putting on a tracksuit, when everyone knows all they really want is a platform for self-promotion. Kenny's different.

TOMMY SMITH on Dalglish's appointment as Liverpool player-manager, **1985**.

He would make a perfect trade union official.

GRAEME SOUNESS in *No Half Measures*, **1985**.

Tommy Docherty

All this talk about Tommy Docherty not being fit to run a football club is rubbish. That's *exactly* what he's fit for.

CLIVE JAMES, **1979**.

If Tommy Docherty survives at Derby, it will be a remarkable feat. But he won't do it through his gift for repartee and off-the-cuff insults.

DEREK DOUGAN, former Northern Ireland international, **1979**. By 1984, Dougan and Docherty were respectively chairman and manager at Wolves.

He's gone 200 years too late.

FIRST-DIVISION MANAGER on Docherty's move to Australia, **1981**.

Tommy Docherty criticising Charlie Nicholas is like Bernard Manning telling Jimmy Tarbuck to clean up his act.

GORDON TAYLOR, players' union secretary, replying to Docherty's remarks on Nicholas's 'indiscipline', **1984**.

His interests are limited to say the least. At home he never read anything in the newspapers but the sports pages. His knowledge of what goes on outside football is so restricted that he couldn't understand why he kept getting into trouble for parking on double yellow lines. He thought they were a new form of street decoration.

CATHERINE LOCKLEY, Docherty's daughter, **1981**.

Peter Doherty

I could run for ever, but even though he was nearly forty Doherty would pass me three times on the way. He was so fit we used to tell him he should be back in the team. We enjoyed working out set-pieces with him, drawing on his ingenuity in devising new moves for free-kicks and throw-ins. But mainly we reacted to his sheer enjoyment of the game.

DANNY BLANCHFLOWER in Tony Pawson, *The Football Managers*, **1973**.

Joe Fagan

Joe doesn't explode very often, but when he does everyone runs for cover.

GRAEME SOUNESS, **1983**.

Ally MacLeod

I think Ally MacLeod believes tactics are a new kind of peppermint.

SCOTLAND PLAYER, **1978**.

When you talk as much as he does, none of it can mean very much.

RON GREENWOOD, England manager, **1978**.

Joe Mercer

Clearly Joe was impressed by the Brazilian defensive formation in which four men were strung in a line across the field. The play of Sheffield United the following season indicated that he decided to incorporate and improve the Brazilian defensive tactics. He did it in a novel and startling fashion. For Joe, if I read United's style of play correctly, added a *fifth* back to the four employed by the Brazilians.

STAN CULLIS, Wolves manager, on the lessons of the 1958 World Cup in *All for the Wolves*, **1960**.

When Joe Mercer and I were friends no one in football could live with us. Between us we had it all. I charged into situations like a bull, full of aggressive ambition and a contempt for anyone who might be standing in my way. And Joe came behind me, picking up the pieces, soothing the wounded and the offended with that vast charm.

MALCOLM ALLISON in *Colours of My Life*, **1975**.

Joe always had style. Everybody loved him; he had a nice friendly way of beating you, a nice gentle way of getting his own way.

FRED EYRE, Manchester City's first-ever apprentice in he 1960s, from *Kicked into Touch*, **1981**.

The first time I met him I knew he was a star, a man who had been given so much more than the natural ability. . .to become a merely famous footballer. There was a puckish humour which cut through the pompous like a knife stroke. There were biting, colourful phrases which rolled off his tongue on their way from a great fund of shrewdness and knowledge of life.

MALCOLM ALLISON in *Colours of My Life*, **1975**.

He quickly lost the one attitude to the game which had disappointed me when I first met him. He had initially been obsessed with aggressive play. I told him that in my opinion he had got the game out of context, especially with his own deep instincts for good, cultured football. And Joe's lapse, given his experience (at Aston Villa), was commendably brief.

MALCOLM ALLISON in *Colours of My Life*, **1975**.

Terry Neill

I've had four top-class managers in Greenwood, Ramsey, Nicholson and now Bond. I want to have some of their qualities, though I hope none of Terry Neill creeps in.

MARTIN PETERS, **1979**.

Bill Nicholson

I did not enjoy dancing around waving trophies in the air. I'm sure he did not like it either. His comments regarding success were always cold, much colder than mine. I was embarrassed by the boasting around us, but I escaped it with humour. He gruffed his way out of it. Our satisfaction was in doing the job.

DANNY BLANCHFLOWER on their partnership.

Frank O'Farrell

I look upon Frank as my last great signing, possibly the greatest of the lot.

SIR MATT BUSBY, on appointing O'Farrell manager of Manchester United, **1971**.

He came like a stranger, and went like a stranger.

DENIS LAW, who played for United under O'Farrell in early **1970s**.

Willie Ormond

Ormond, to many senior players, was too nice a man to be a successful international manager. . .Donny Osmond was one of the nick-names he was given.

DANNY McGRAIN, Celtic and Scotland captain, in *Celtic – My Team*, **1978**.

Willie never gave us talks about foreign teams, because he couldn't pronounce their names. But once in Scandinavia he stopped us as we were going out and said, 'Watch out for the big blond at corners and free kicks.' So we went out onto the field and looked across at them, and there were about six big blonds. Well, we were playing Sweden.

SCOTLAND PLAYER, **1974**.

Bob Paisley

He's broken this silly myth that nice guys don't win anything. He's one of the nicest guys you could meet in any industry or any walk of life – and he's a winner.

BRIAN CLOUGH, **1978**.

Sir Alf Ramsey

Some respected, knowledgeable observers feel that Ramsey has serious shortcomings as a manager. At the same time there are many people inside football who have enormous, unequivocal admiration for Ramsey the manager. A few find him flawless; most admit he has deficiencies, but some of these consider them unimportant beside his qualities. The same could be said for Rasputin.

MAX MARQUIS, *Anatomy of a Football Manager*, **1970**.

It is clear that Ramsey is self-conscious to a highly inhibitory degree about his elocution. In public he lets words go through a tightly controlled mouth; his eyes move uneasily. Yet he is to be no more blamed or mocked for his speech than someone who cannot sing in tune. . . . If this were not enough, his words are noted down meticulously and used in evidence against him.

MAX MARQUIS, *Anatomy of a Football Manager*, **1970**.

He is the most patriotic man I have ever met.

GEOFF HURST, Ramsey's centre-forward in **1966** World Cup final.

We've all followed Ramsey. The winger was dead once you played four defenders. Alf saw that in 1966 and it just took the rest of us a little longer to understand.

DAVE BOWEN, Wales manager, in Tony Pawson, *The Football Managers*, **1973**.

There's no substitute for skill, but the manager's job is usually to find one. Ramsey obviously found one.

GEORGE RAYNOR, in Max Marquis, *Anatomy of a Football Manager*, **1970**.

Ramsey recognized that the real strengths and values of English football were embodied not by Trevor Brooking, but by Nobby Stiles. Ramsey was right.

EAMON DUNPHY, **1981**.

As a manager, Alf Ramsey is like a good chicken farmer. If a hen doesn't lay, a good chicken farmer rings its neck.

JACKIE MILBURN, journalist, formerly Newcastle United and England centre-forward of the 1940s and 50s.

He is more careful of his aspirates than his answers.

ARTHUR HOPCRAFT, journalist.

Dear Sir Alf, For what it's worth we'd like to say thankyou. Thankyou for bringing English football back from the débâcle of Hungary at Wembley to the very top drawer. Thankyou for creating an environment where players like the Charltons, Moore, Hunter, Hurst and Banks could blossom and delight. Thankyou for leaving your job with the same dignity and decorum that you always showed whilst in it. From the brewers of Watney Red.

WATNEY advertisement, **1974**.

Don Revie

It has been said that Revie got rid of all the rebels and only kept in the good guys but that is not in keeping with his record at Leeds, or in his early days with England. He had this fatherly way with players that led to his nickname 'The Godfather'.

TREVOR BROOKING in *An Autobiography*, **1981**.

Don Revie's appointment as England manager was a classic example of poacher turning gamekeeper.

ALAN HARDAKER in *Hardaker of the League*, **1977**.

It makes me angry to hear criticism of a man who is working himself into the ground and trying all he knows to get things right for the England team. All the man needs is a break.

DICK WRAGG, chairman of the FA international committee, defending Don Revie in Rio de Janeiro shortly before Revie's defection to Dubai, **1977**.

He was an utterly brilliant manager, but knotted with fear.

GARY SPRAKE, ex-Leeds goalkeeper.

Bobby Robson

His natural expression is that of a man who fears he might have left the gas on.

DAVID LACEY in the *Guardian*, **1985**.

Ron Saunders

He'll never forgive Bob Geldof for thinking of Live Aid before him.

MIDLANDS journalist on Birmingham manager's Save Our Society campaign, **1985**.

Bill Shankly

I believe Bill Shankly died of a broken heart after he stopped managing Liverpool and saw them go on to even greater success without him. Giving your whole life to a football club is a sad mistake.

JOHN GILES on his return to the manager's chair at West Bromwich Albion, **1984**.

Jock Stein

John, you're immortal.

BILL SHANKLY to Stein in Celtic dressing-room after European Cup final victory over Inter Milan, **1967**.

Peter Taylor

I'm not equipped to manage successfully without him [Peter Taylor]. I am the shop front. He is the goods in the back. Peter's strength is that he has the ability to see things twenty-four hours before I do. I like time if the decision has to be right. In assessing a player, for example, I like three weeks. Peter often has to do it in ninety minutes.

BRIAN CLOUGH, **1973**.

We pass each other on the A52 going to work on most days of the week. But if his car broke down and I saw him thumbing a lift, I wouldn't pick him up – I'd run him over.

CLOUGH after the break-up of the partnership, **1983**.

Howard Wilkinson

He turned down a job in Saudi Arabia because they couldn't guarantee any hills for the players to run up and down.

MIKE LYONS, Sheffield Wednesday defender, on his manager's notorious training routines, **1985**.

Walter Winterbottom

Before one match against Wales, Walter got out the blackboard and outlined exactly what he wanted done from the kick-off. 'Milburn will pass the ball back to Wright. He will play it wide to Finney, Milburn and Mortensen will make dummy runs into the penalty area but Finney will cut inside and play it to Shackleton on the edge of the box, and Shackleton will kick it into the net.' I looked at him and said, 'Which side, Walter, left or right?' He was not amused, and although we beat Wales 4–1 I never played for England again for five years.

LEN SHACKLETON, former Sunderland forward and an international of the **1940s** and **50s**.

Because I play for England he thinks I understand peripheral vision and positive running.

JIMMY GREAVES, **1960**.

Billy Wright

We all liked him, but you cannot help taking advantage. Footballers are tough competitors by nature. They are trained to walk over people. If he lets them they'll make a doormat of the manager as well as opponents.

TERRY NEILL, Arsenal captain, later club manager, on the 1966 sacking of Wright in Tony Pawson, *The Football Managers*, **1973**.

3

The Game That Was

Forasmuch as there is great noise in the city caused by hustling over large balls, from which many evils may arise, which God forbid, we command and forbid on behalf of the King, on pain of imprisonment, such game to be used in the city in future.

EDWARD II, proclamation banning football, **1314**.

No foteball player be used or suffered within the City of London and the liberties thereof upon pain of imprisonment.

QUEEN ELIZABETH I, proclamation, **1572**.

Footeballe is a pastime to be utterly objected by all noble men, the game giving no pleasure, but beastlie furie and violence.

SIR THOMAS ELYOT, **1579**.

Lord, remove these exercises from the Sabaoth. Any exercise which withdraweth from godliness either upon the Sabaoth or on any other day, is wicked and to be forbidden.

PHILLIP STUBBES, *Anatome of Abuses in the Realme of England*, **1583**. Stubbes, a Puritan, saw football as a 'devilishe pastime'.

They have the sleights to meet one betwixt two, to dash him against the hart with their elbowes, to butt him under the short ribs with their griped fists, and with their knees to catch him on the hip and pick him on his neck, with a hundred such murthering devices. . . .

PHILLIP STUBBES, on the early art of tackling.

For as concerning football playing, I protest unto you it may be rather called a friendlie kinde of fyghte than a play or recreation, a bloody or murthuring practise than a felowly sporte or pastime.

PHILLIP STUBBES.

That whereas there has been heretofore great disorders in our town of Manchester, and the inhabitants thereof greatly wronged and charged with makinge and amendinge of their glasse windows broken yearelye and spoyled by a companye of lewd and disordered persons using that unlawfull exercise of playinge with the ffote-ball in ye streets of ye sd towne breakinge many men's windowes and glasse at their plesures and other great enormities. Therefore we of this jury doe order that no manner of persons hereafter shall play or use the ffote-ball in any street within the said towne of Manchester.

MANCHESTER LETE ROLL, **1608**.

In winter foot-ball is a useful and charming exercise. It is a leather ball about as big as one's head, filled with wind. This kick'd about from one to t'other in the streets, by him that can get it, and that is all the art of it.

J. MISSON, *Memoirs and Observations of M. Misson in His Travels over England*, **1697**.

In cold weather you sometimes see a score of rascals in the streets kicking at a ball, and they will break panes of glass and smash the windows of coaches, and will also knock you down without the slightest compunction; on the contrary they will roar with laughter.

CÉSAR DE SAUSSURE, 'Letter from England', **1728**.

The game was formerly much in vogue among the common people though of late years it seems to have fallen into disrepute and is but little practised.

JOSEPH STRUTT, historian, **1801**.

Put out of the game any player wilfully breaking any of the football rules.

HARROW SCHOOL, direction to umpires, pre-**1860**.

A player is considered to be 'sneaking' when only three, or less than three, of the opposite side are before him and the ball behind him, and in such case he may not kick the ball.

ETON SCHOOL football rule, pre-**1860**.

What happens when a game of football is proposed at Christmas among a party of young men assembled from different schools? Alas! We have seen the attempt made again and again, but invariably with a failure as the result. The Eton man is enamoured of his own rules, and turns his nose up at Rugby as not sufficiently aristocratic; while the Rugbeian retorts that 'bullying' and 'sneaking' are not to his taste, and he is not afraid of his shins, or of a 'maul' or 'scrimmage'. On hearing this the Harrovian pricks up his ears, and though he might previously have sided with Rugby, the insinuation against the courage of those who do not allow 'shinning' arouses his ire, and causes him to refuse to play with one who has offered it. Thus it is found impossible to get up a game.

THE FIELD, Editorial, December **1861**.

Rule 3: Kicks must be aimed only at the ball.

J. C. THRING, The Simplest Game (rules of football), **1862**.

But why should the Blackheath men insist on hacking? It is clearly an evil, though in some games (the Rugby game for instance) a necessary evil. In any game played according to the new rules there seems no necessity for it, and there will always be enough casual hacking to satisfy the most bloodthirsty man that ever fought for or on Blackheath. Why should not Blackheath effect a compromise, retaining tripping-up, and any casual hack they may get, and abandon all theoretical hacking?

A RUGBEIAN, letter to *The Field*, December **1863**. Blackheath's representative at the formation of the Football Association maintained that carrying the ball and hacking were vital principles of their game. The club could not join if it was excluded from the rules.

A dangerous and painful practice, very brutal when deliberate and likely to prevent a man who had due regard for his wife and family from following the game.

A. PEMBER, the first FA president, appealing to Blackheath to abandon hacking, **1863**.

If we have hacking, no-one who has arrived at the years of discretion will play at football, and it will be entirely relinquished to school-boys.

E. C. MORLEY, FA secretary, **1863**.

They had no right to draw up such a rule at Cambridge and that it savours far more of the feelings of those who liked their pipes and grog or schnapps more than the manly games of football. . . .If you do away with hacking you will do away with all the courage and pluck of the game, and I will be bound to bring over a lot of Frenchmen who would beat you with a week's practice.

F. W. CAMPBELL, Blackheath secretary, **1863**.

If anybody thinks I care about shinning, let them give me a kick and try. They'll find it a game two can play at, and I shall not be at all likely to stop and look at the law and see whether shinning is allowed: not I.

We've just been playing a match – it was awfully jolly, I got lots of kicks. It was what we call a 'big little' (i.e. not limited to the crack men) match, and a lot of the fellows' fathers, and mothers, and sisters were there to see. The girls squeaked a bit when they saw their brothers upset, because it is 'in their nature to do so'; but you never hear a fellow squeak even if his leg is broken.

A PUBLIC SCHOOLBOY of the third form, letter to *The Field*, December **1863**.

Despite all that has been recently said about 'hacking', 'mauling' and 'shinning', we feel bound to add that football teaches *forebearance*. If, as Plato says, 'a boy is the most vicious of all wild beasts', the taming and training process begins very early and does its work well. We have seen boys playing football resist great temptations and guard lesser boys from wrong. We have also seen them give way to temptation, and manifest immediately afterwards a deep regret and repentance which most assuredly contraverted the Platonian dictum.

JOHN D. CARTWRIGHT, 'Football – The Value of the Game', in *The Field*, October **1863**.

No player shall be allowed to wear projecting nails, iron plates, or gutta percha on the soles or heels of his boots.

LAW 14, Football Association rules, **1863**.

I would earnestly beg all who have any voice or influence in deciding on or forwarding this question to remember that it is the interests of *all* classes of the people, not of the public school boys or gentlemen players only, that have to be considered.

A HALLAMSHIRE MAN, letter to *The Field*, December **1863**, on the great football rules debate.

Football is a gentleman's game played by hooligans, and rugby a hooligan's game played by gentlemen.

ANON, though often attributed to an unnamed chancellor of Cambridge University, late nineteenth century.

It is a good plan, if it can previously be so arranged, to have one side with striped jerseys of one colour, say red; and the other with another, say blue. This prevents confusion and wild attempts to run after and wrest the ball from your neighbour. I have often seen this done, and heard the invariable apology – 'I beg your pardon, I thought you were on the opposite side.'

ROUTLEDGE'S HANDBOOK OF FOOTBALL, **1867**.

This club shall be called the Queen's Park Football Club and its object shall be the recreation and amusement of its members.

QUEEN'S PARK, constitution, **1867**.

SHE: I'm afraid Arthur will some day come home with a broken leg.
HE: Don't be alarmed, for if he does it will not be his own.

EXCHANGE, between Mrs (later Lady) Kinnaird and Major (later Sir) Francis Marindin, on her husband, in the **1870s**.

CHARLES ALCOCK (Old Harrovians captain): Look here, Kinnaird, are we going to play the game, or are we going to have hacking?
ARTHUR KINNAIRD (Old Etonians captain): Oh, let us have hacking by all means.

PRE-MATCH EXCHANGE in the **1870s**.

What has been the recreation of a few is now becoming the pursuit of thousands, an athletic exercise carried on under a strict system and in many cases by an enforced term of training, almost magnified into a profession.

CHARLES ALCOCK, captain of The Wanderers, the first FA Cup winners in **1872**, later the first paid FA secretary.

The great majority of players were snobs from the south who had no use for a lawyer from Sheffield. The ball was never passed to him and nobody ever spoke to him. . . . They did not understand him and he resented their air of superiority.

SIR FREDERICK WALL, on Charles Clegg's one England appearance in **1872**.

I fear we shall not be able to get up any 'foreign' matches, the good example set here not having been taken up in other parts of the Presidency. I believe the game is being tried in Kurrachee, Scinde, where in winter the climate is cold enough to warrant it; but a three days' journey is rather too much to take for a game played on sand, there being no turf in those benighted regions.

WILLIAM PATERSON (Old Rugbeian), letter to *The Field* on the problems of the Bombay FC, September **1872**.

We started off in the forenoon to walk to the ground – a distance of nearly five miles; but after reaching our destination found that there was no chance of getting inside the ground unless we paid at the gate. What few coppers we had had among us were gone by this time, and how disappointed we felt, after such a weary walk, at the poor prospect of our getting a view of the game. Just when we had given up all hope, we earnestly begged a cabman to accommodate us on the top of his cab, and it was from that perch I witnessed the first encounter between the two nations.

W. ARNOTT, Scotland full-back, on his visit as a 10-year old to the first Scotland v. England game in 1872.

We are sorry to say that, during a football match played between St Bartholomew's Hospital and the University College Schools on Saturday last at Victoria Park, two very serious accidents occurred. . . . One student had his leg broken, the other his ankle dislocated. It is further stated that others of the competitors were very roughly mauled, especially in the neighbourhood of their shins. Football accidents have been by far too common of late. . . . Rugby, we fear, must be responsible for setting a bad example.

The Lancet, December 1872.

Arthur Dunn taught us to play football as honourably as the game of life, to recite the Kings of Judah and Israel, to love God and to hate Harrow.

SIR SHANE LESLIE, Memoir of Arthur Dunn, Old Etonians and England player of the 1880s and 1890s and later headmaster of Ludgrove School.

In the North of England. . .the game is often played in a very different spirit, and at times the anxiety to win leads to much unpleasantness.

The Field, 1882.

The working population must be amused – is it to be the football field, or the dram shop?

Scottish Athletic Journal, 1883.

FAN: Is't that t'Cup? Why it's like a tea kettle.
'Ey lad, but it's very welcome in Lancashire. It'll have a good home and it'll ne'er go back to London.

S. A. WARBURTON, Blackburn Olympic captain, after winning the FA Cup against the Old Etonians, **1883**.

The game of football, as originally played at the Wall at Eton, was the author of every sort and condition of football now played throughout the United Kingdom.

The Etonian, November **1884**.

The admission into the amateur ranks of professional football players is possibly the beginning of the end in an important social movement with which everybody must sympathise. The idea has been to bring together all classes in football and athletics on terms of perfect equality. With the introduction of professionals a new departure is taken. The first effect of the change will be to make the Rugby game the aristocratic one, and the Association game will probably almost die out in the South of England, where it is already declining in favour.

Manchester Guardian, November **1884**.

£1 per week should be ample remuneration for the best professional footballer that ever existed.

Football Field, a Bolton-based soccer paper, January **1886**.

Are you all Englishmen? Then I have very much pleasure in presenting you with the ball. You have played a very good game and I hope you will win the Cup.

MAJOR MARINDIN, FA president, to West Bromwich players after refereeing **1886** semi-final *v.* Preston, who had several Scots in their team.

The narrow squeaks that Scotchmen have had in the last two or three internationals have convinced me that English football is now quite on a par with the Scots.

'FORWARD', writing in *The Scottish Umpire*, **1887**.

I believe all right-minded people have good reason to thank God for the great progress of this popular national game.

ARTHUR KINNAIRD, Old Etonians captain.

The professional or semi-professional player does not as a rule delight in hard-charging like the Eton schoolboys, but he well understands the way to bring down his man with an artful trip, while escaping the notice of the referee.

Baily's Magazine, **1891**.

It was agreed to buy for the players, after the match, half a bottle of whisky and one bottle of port, and to treat the visiting players to a pie and a pint of ale apiece.

FORFAR ATHLETIC Minute Book, **1890**.

Sheffield are beaten already. They are down in the dumps and sitting in the dressing-room quiet as mice. They have not a word to say. They look frightened. But the Rovers are singing and whistling and carrying on like a lot of kittens. Unless I am very much mistaken they will win easily.

R. P. GREGSON, Lancashire secretary, before the **1890** FA Cup final. Blackburn won 6–1.

The Rangers' football was not lamb-like, which is possibly why the Corinthians enjoyed the game.

C. B. FRY, on Rangers *v*. Corinthians at Ibrox, **1890s**.

Moon had come a long way out of goal and had taken the ball off a forward's toe, and punted it away, and was returning to goal when the forward deliberately assisted him with a distinct hoof. It may only have been the Scotchman's way of showing his appreciation of the save, but Billy saw it in a different light and chased him. The referee saved further bloodshed.

C. B. FRY on the same match.

He remarked that last year he was in the South of France and one morning when bringing the coffee the waiter spoke to him of the Wolverhampton Wanderers, observing that they were doing very well.

MAYOR OF WOLVERHAMPTON, to the Town Council, 27 March **1893**.

It [football] does not make trained soldiers of our young men, it is true, but it enhances in them the spirit of pluck, opposition, competition, never-know-when-they-are-beaten, play up Wednesday or United kind of feeling, which tends to the greatness of our national character. Long live football!

Football World, a Sheffield paper, greeting the **1895–96** season.

The artisan differs from the public school man in two important points; he plays to win at all costs and from the nature of his associations, he steps onto the football field in better training.

Badminton Magazine, **1896**.

The tour is ill-conceived. The FA are sending professionals to play against university men.

N. L. ('PA') JACKSON, founder of the Corinthians, on the FA's first foreign tour, to Germany in **1899**.

Strange to relate, the professionals managed to behave themselves.

Athletic News report on the tour.

The team's successes in the Cup-ties were appreciated by the public in a way that was, to put it mildly, detrimental to the players, who were encouraged to excess in every direction. Some of the men had not the moral courage to resist this mistaken kindness, and as a result they have had to seek pastures new.

TOTTENHAM HOTSPUR Handbook, **1899/1900**.

The aggressiveness of the professional element asserted itself in many ways. Not content with almost filling the international teams with professionals, it did all in its power to reduce the one or two amateurs who did play to the level of the professionals. All were taken to the same hotel, all were expected to travel together, and all were asked to feed together.

N. L. ('PA') JACKSON, **1900**.

After playing in a Rugby match some weeks ago I developed an irritable infection of the scalp which has hitherto baffled my doctor, in spite of ointments and internal treatment. The complaint, which is clearly contagious, appeared first in the shape of a small boil, which hardened until a loose crust appeared and this, being dispersed, spread the trouble further. The parts most affected are those which were rubbed in the course of the game. I should be glad to know if I am suffering from 'football impetigo', and if so what treatment should be adopted. I shall then be enabled to enlighten my medico and perhaps benefit others.

RUGBEIAN, letter to *The Field*, March **1900**.

I have just asked one of the Bury players if he was not very tired and his answer was 'I am very dry.'

LORD ROSEBERY, during presentation of the FA Cup to Bury, **1903**.

The League Committee's decision is to disqualify Christov for a year and let off Sharples with a 'caution'! This year we have Sharples the Throttler! Next we shall have Jim the Stabber and Jack the Ripper! Match reports will soon read like crime records. Will that gladden the hearts of Russian sportsmen? Certainly not. The British, in their typical high-handed manner, with their big voting majority, are banning a Russian who is totally blameless and letting off a man who is obviously dangerous but is one of their own.

Moscow Sport in **1903** after an English referee had sent off a Russian player for a tackle on an Englishman. (The league was made up exclusively of foreign residents' clubs).

There is a daily increasing tendency for clubs to look askance at men who have not a clean record. Clubs have begun to learn – nay, they have learned! – that it does not take many black sheep to lead the whole flock astray. So long as I am connected with football I shall never sanction the admission into any team of a man who has not a clean record. It is all very well to be a fine footballer; but the man who can play good football and is occasionally unfit to do so, is of doubtful value to a side.

WILLIAM ISIAH BASSETT, West Bromwich Albion director and former England winger, in 'The Day's Work: How the Professional Footballer is Trained', *The Book of Football*, **1906**.

I do not like to see footballers getting £4 a week – or even £3, if you like – slouching about in mufflers and dispensing with collars. It brings the game into contempt with the very class we want to draw to our matches.

BASSETT, as above.

Their football, although of a different type, may have been equally fine, but underlying it has been the thought that it was a business first and a pleasure second. It is human nature that it should be so.

The Times, contrasting the great professional clubs with the Corinthains in **1909**.

Constant practice, and the living of a strictly temperate life, go to make not only the skilful but the enduring footballer.

BASSETT in *The Book of Football*, **1906**.

'Sy, Bill, where's this 'ere Bury wot's playing Sahth-ampton?' It was a Cockney lad who asked the question of his mate as he gazed in wonder on the enthusiastic mob of Lancashire men swarming up the Strand. Bill had to confess ignorance of the precise geographical position of the place in question, and the nearest he could hazard was 'Dahn norf somewheres.'

WILLIAM PICKFORD and ALFRED GIBSON, on the 1900 FA Cup final, *Association Football and the Men Who Made It*, **1906**.

The inhabitants are interested in coal mining and football, if they're male; having babies and looking after their menfolk, if they are female. Monotonous? Perhaps when judged by modern standards of television, of 'H' bombs and of skiffle groups, but when I was born, a few years before the Great War, there seemed little of importance outside Orbiston.

MATT BUSBY, on his 1909 Scottish birthplace, in *My Story*, **1957**.

Goalkeepers do not grow on trees. That is a truism, no doubt, yet many people imagine that custodians of the sticks are as plentiful as berries in autumn.

J. W. ROBINSON, 'How to Keep Goal' in Pickford and Gibson, **1906**.

In the last dozen years there has been a great change in the character of the paid player. . . . We now see him able to take his position in the best of company, and would have no hesitation in asking a lady to take a seat with him in his saloon. Why, it is a fact that the Manchester City team on our recent journey to London for the final of the English Cup, surprised the occupants of a station they were leaving by singing, and that too quite musically, 'Lead, Kindly Light'.

WILLIAM (BILLY) MEREDITH, 'Impressions of Wing Play' in Pickford and Gibson, **1906**.

In answer to Berks & Bucks FA, the Council decided that there could be no objection to a player with a wooden leg taking part in the game, provided he did not play in a manner dangerous to his opponents.

MINUTE 21 of FA Council meeting, March **1907**.

Don't think because you are on the stand you have a right to shout instructions at the players. They know what to do without any assistance from you.

Don't snap your neighbour's nose off because he thinks differently from you. You have come to see your side win, and he has perhaps come to see the other.

Don't make yourself a nuisance to those around you by continually bellowing at the top of your voice, it gets on people's nerves and takes away a lot of the enjoyment of the game, besides making yourself look ridiculous.

SHEFFIELD UNITED programme, October **1907**.

The Football Association is composed of autocrats who demand that we shall surrender our rights of citizenship. We must not go to law without first obtaining permission, they themselves clinging like limpets to the privilege of suspending and punishing us – without allowing us to appear and plead our case before them.

WILLIAM (BILLY) MEREDITH, *The Clarion*, **1909**.

If William (Billy) Meredith thinks the public are with the Players' Union he is sadly mistaken. I come across very few who do not think footballers are amply paid at £4 a week. . . .

C. E. SUTCLIFFE, *Athletic News*, March **1909**, on proposed players' strike.

> Han we lost afore we'en started?
> Han we heck! We'st win today!
> We'en a team of gradely triers –
> As they fund deawn Ashton road
> An' fro' th' top o' th' League to th' bottom
> We're noan as feeart as what they're coed.

POEM welcoming Newcastle to Boundary Park for Oldham's first home match in the First Division, **1910**.

Were cricket and football abolished, it would bring upon the masses nothing but misery, depression, sloth, indiscipline and disorder.

LORD BIRKENHEAD, *Pastime*, **1911**.

It is to be hoped that the picture of two detestable young women wearing stuffed robins in their hats as a 'compliment' to the Swindon football team is a libel and an invention. The footballers who call themselves by the name of our popular little red-breast can hardly be gratified by seeing the dead bodies of their mascot stuck on girls' heads; and if they possess the ordinary, healthy instinct of young Englishmen are more likely to hiss the wearers off the ground than to wish to walk out with them on Sunday.

(MISS) L. SARDINER, Secretary, Royal Society for the Protection of Birds, in letter to the *Swindon Evening Advertiser*, **1912**.

The clubs and their supporters have seen the Cup played for, and now it is their duty to join with each other and play a sterner game for England.

LORD DERBY, presenting FA Cup to Sheffield United, **1915**.

Now then my man, we want none of that [swearing].
Thee! Thee fuck off!

INTERCHANGE between A. G. Baiche Bower, the last amateur to captain England, and his left-back, Bill Ashurst, during England v. Wales match, **1925**.

The outcry against inflated transfer values has been loud and long and some of the loudest have been foremost in the open cheque rush. It is proverbially better to practise than to preach.

CHELSEA programme **1926–27** – a dig at Arsenal, who had called for a limit on fees but spent £25,000 in two years.

Father says I am too smart at multiplication to make a good goal-keeper. Teacher says there is no disgrace in it. . . . I am expecting a gold watch from Miss Cicely Courtnidge, the actress, being the boy who has let more goals pass him than anyone else we know of.

DONALD MATTHEWS PRATLEY, aged twelve, goalkeeper for Raglan Elementary School, North London, **1929**. Raglan's record was played 20, lost 20; goals for 6, against 269.

If insanity is to continue in this matter, then we will be insane with the rest.

ARSENAL programme editorial, **1931**, after reproach by Chelsea over spiralling transfer fees.

I cannot consider the game of football at all gentlemanly; after all, the Yorkshire common people play it.

The Old Etonian, **1931**.

Even then he must have had a horror of professionalism, for as they went on to the field I said, 'Half a sovereign for every goal, Edgar.' 'Money for playing football?' he queried with a frown on his young face.

F. B. DOUGLAS-HAMILTON, on the fourteen-year old Edgar Kail – later an England international though still an amateur – in *The Boy's Own Annual*, **1933–34**.

Clubs cannot do just as they like – even if they desire floodlight football. That must be in the future. I cannot easily predict an era when the sorcerers of science may easily turn night into day as they now talk to a man on the other side of the world.

SIR FREDERICK WALL, FA chairman, **1935**.

It is rather old fashioned now, because it was old when I left off 'footer' – 14 years ago – but still, as you know, the old-fashioned recipes are usually the best. Take about two ounces of beeswax and pare it finely into an old jar. Pour on half a pint of neatsfoot oil, and place the jar by the fire. Let the oil simmer until the wax is dissolved stirring all the time. It is then ready for use. The neatsfoot oil acts as a fine preservative for the leather, and beeswax helps greatly to keep out the water. Just try it, boys – there'll be no more stiff boots nor wasted money.

E. W. HARMER, 'Those Football Boots: A Useful Tip', in *The Boy's Own Annual*, **1936–37**.

4

The Beautiful Game

Styles, Standards and Lifestyles

There's no rule to say a game can't finish 9–9.

GRAHAM TAYLOR, Watford manager, after 7–3 defeat at Nottingham Forest, **1982**.

There is no FIFA rule that says teams cannot play as they please.

HERMANN NEUBURGER, German FA president, after uncompetitive West Germany-Austria match which took both teams into the quarter-finals of the **1982** World Cup.

In football it is widely acknowledged that if both sides agree to cheat, cheating is fair.

C. B. FRY, **1911**.

The beauty of soccer, the reason why I think it is the best team game of all, is that there are so many factors outside the control of a coach. If a coach could control a soccer game, it would become very boring indeed. In American Football the play becomes just an extension of the will and imagination of the two coaches. This can be fascinating, sure, but I'm not certain it has much to do with sport, certainly as Europeans know sport.

JOHN GILES, Vancouver Whitecaps coach, in James Lawton, *The All American War Game*, **1984**.

You ought to get a bunch of clowns if you just want entertainment.

ALAN DURBAN, Stoke manager, answering criticisms of his team's negative display at Arsenal, **1980**.

You can argue for hours, without reaching a conclusion favourable to all, about whether football is an art or a sport. Some of the taller brows feel that what really matters in the end is the style of the performance, but professional football is also a business and the average fan in Scotland wants, first and foremost, to see his team win. But while realizing that football in Scotland is a mixture of so many different methods I must say that I prefer the graceful approach and I believe that pure skill and craftsmanship will always triumph over more enthusiastic, brawny tactics.

GORDON SMITH, one of Hibernian's 'Famous Five' forward line of the 1950s, in Hugh Taylor, *Great Masters of Scottish Football*, **1968**.

The great fallacy is that the game is first and last about winning. It's nothing of the kind. The game is about glory. It's about doing things in style, with a flourish, about going out and beating the other lot, not waiting for them to die of boredom.

DANNY BLANCHFLOWER in Hunter Davies, *The Glory Game*, **1972**.

Football in Britain is divided because our society is divided. The old communal joy has gone. The man in charge of our wolf clubs' teams in Belfast was not a coach, but he loved football. On Sunday mornings he would read out the match reports of the previous day's games. He made football a romance, and above all else, that is what the game should be.

DANNY BLANCHFLOWER, **1983**.

Football is a simple game. The hard part is making it look simple.

RON GREENWOOD, England manager, **1978**.

A centre-forward should be thinking about goal as soon as he leaves the centre circle, and his shot should be hitting goal as soon as he arrives at the penalty area.

JOCK DODDS, Blackpool's war-time No. 9, in Robin Daniels, *Blackpool Football*, **1972**.

Football is the ultimate in team sport, and no individual can win a game by himself. Pele is a famous name, but Pele made his goals because another player passed to him at the proper time. And Brazil won games because Pele didn't try to make the goals by himself, but passed to others when required so that the goal could be scored.

PELE in *My Life and the Beautiful Game*, **1977**.

The world's best eleven players wouldn't make a team. You must have blend.

LEN SHACKLETON, *Clown Prince of Soccer*, **1955**.

It is a mistake to enter a game with fixed ideas on tactics. If you are a half-back the first thing you should find out is the sort of form each front-line man happens to be in, and then see to it that the fellows on top of their game see most of the ball.

SYD BISHOP, West Ham wing-half, **1924**.

You just cannot tell star players how they must play and what they must do when they are on the field in an international match. You must let them play their natural game, which has paid big dividends in the past. I have noticed that in recent years these pre-match instructions have become more and more long-winded while the playing ability of the players on the field has dwindled.

STANLEY MATTHEWS in *The Stanley Matthews Story*, **1960**.

Good captains, like dinosaurs, are threatened with extinction. They are being hounded into a state of nervous nonentity by a huge pack of master minds who inhabit the higher, drier lands of the grandstands.

DANNY BLANCHFLOWER in *The Encyclopedia of Association Football*, **1960**.

How do I prefer to play? However they tell me – you do a lot for
a cap you know. I've played it long out of defence, chipped out
of defence, carried it out of defence. And if I couldn't see anyone
to give it to, I belted it out of sight. In this game you do what
you're told.

JIMMY DICKINSON, Portsmouth and England player, **1940–60s**.

The only thing I enjoyed during my six years at Middlesbrough
was scoring goals. From Saturday to Saturday I was very unhappy.
My ability was never utilized, by me or the management. Only
goals kept me sane. That was the only pleasure.

BRIAN CLOUGH, **1973**.

Walter Winterbottom stereotyped players. The coaching manuals
produced sixty-one ways of trapping the ball, whereas there might
have been 189 – George Wardle at Cardiff used to trap the ball
with his backside all the time. Now I once saw a film with Eddie
Cantor. There were two hypnotists and one said to the other: 'I
see you're reading the same book on hypnotism as I am. What
chapter have you reached?' 'Chapter 4,' said the other. 'Oh, I've
reached Chapter 8,' replied the first, 'you are now in my
command.' Coaching footballers became like that.

HARRY MAY, Cardiff, Barnsley, Swindon and Southend player in the **1950s**.

It is easy to lock the stable door after the horse has gone, but I
believe the only way to beat this tactical system of the Continentals
is by playing the Arsenal type of defensive system. . . . If the
Hungarians or any other team have the ball in midfield, let them
have it. They have got to get to our penalty area to score goals,
because that is where the goal is, and to win matches goals must
be scored. . . . I believe that if our team, attack and defence,
retreat to our eighteen-yard line and let the Hungarians come to
us, we are compact and as soon as their attack is 'broken down',
then is the time for us to assume the attack (defenders and
attackers together) using the square ball and then the through
one, which the Continentals are now doing.

TOMMY LAWTON, Arsenal and England centre-forward, in *Soccer the Lawton Way*,
1954.

Those who criticize our current standards in British football might well consider the point. Efficiency – the most dreadful of virtues – we do not possess. But as for charm – it is all ours.

DR PERCY M. YOUNG in *Football Year*, **1956**.

I'm not one of those who says it was better in the old days – the days when we never saw a ball all week in training so that we'd be 'hungry for it' on Saturday. Today, they're better athletes, the players are more mobile, and coaching has made them more efficient. But I don't know. . . . I look at a game like Newcastle against Spurs on telly, and I think what is this – Third Division football or First?

ARTHUR ROWE in *Foul! Book of Football*, **1975**.

I can't believe that English football will ever again be as exciting or as full of outstanding performers as it was when we were in our prime. There was one more great period, after the men we were brought up with were gone, something you could look back on as a sort of golden era. That was when Greaves and Law, Bobby Charlton and Best, the tremendous Tottenham team that did the double and a lot of other class players were around. But real quality has become scarcer and scarcer since the 1960s.

TOM FINNEY, former Preston and England forward, **1983**.

But you cannot have enjoyed it. There were so many mistakes, so much unprofessional play.

SIR ALF RAMSEY to a journalist enthusing over a Stoke *v*. Liverpool match containing five goals. Tony Pawson, *The Football Managers*, **1973**.

Sometimes I hear old-timers scoff at these blackboard tactics. Frankly I can't understand why. . .in these days of defence in depth and a defence complex which threatens to paralyse all attacking ideas, it is absolutely vital to discuss the opposition; their strengths and weaknesses; and also for your own team to have their own pet moves thoroughly worked out.

DON REVIE in *Soccer's Happy Wanderer*, **1956**.

I've never agreed with numbering players. I would like to see it abolished tomorrow. When I've seen wing-halves looking for the numbers they have to mark I think it's terrible. Surely the man you have to mark is the man nearest to you who has got the ball. That's where the danger lies.

TED DRAKE, Chelsea manager, in *The Encyclopedia of Association Football*, **1960**.

Between the ages of twenty-seven and thirty-two, footballers are in their prime. It is from this age-group that teams capable of winning the World Cup should come. If, then, England intend making a serious challenge for 1962 honours, a team of twenty-five to thirty-year-olds should be built up now. The present age-group, from which England is team-building, should reach full maturity in 1966. . .four years too late to win the 1962 World Cup.

JIMMY McILROY, Burnley and Northern Ireland midfield player, in *Right Inside Soccer*, **1960**.

Football's meant to be enjoyed and I still enjoy it, but I probably enjoyed it more at fifteen. The finer points disappeared when England won the World Cup in 1966. Now the object is not to get beat at all costs.

ALAN GILZEAN in Hunter Davies, *The Glory Game*, **1972**.

I got caught up in the work-rate era at Arsenal. My own improved a lot but I lost my sharpness in the box. Finally Bill McGarry came to take me to Wolves with words that were music to me: 'If I see you in our half, I'll kick your arse.'

BOBBY GOULD, striker with nine clubs, **1978**.

What then do I think of English football? Again the answer is simple: 'Not bloody much.' When I first became a professional footballer, like everyone else in Scotland I was brainwashed into believing the hysteria the English media gush out over their Football League. . . . It used to make me mad to read some of the piffle written about the English set-up, but now I just have a good belly-laugh to myself. . .it is so much nonsense.

DANNY McGRAIN, Celtic and Scotland captain, in *Celtic – My Team*, **1978**.

Attack and be damned.

DAVID PLEAT, Luton manager, **1982**.

It is sad, but I no longer enjoy watching football today. Most of the time I find myself looking at my watch and wishing that the referee would blow his whistle and put us out of our misery.

RAICH CARTER, former manager and England international, **1983**.

Make it simple, make it accurate, make it quick.

ARTHUR ROWE.

Our football has suffered in the last twenty-five years through our players being 'typed'. We have had types of players for full-backs; types for wing-halves; types for centre-halves and centre-forwards, tall enough and big enough to bash the daylights out of each other; your inside-forwards have got to supply the craft; the wing-forwards have got to be able to run; full-backs have got to be strong and be able to kick. All of which, of course, is quite wrong. They are all footballers; they should all be fluid and capable players.

ARTHUR ROWE in *The Encyclopedia of Association Football*, **1960**.

Total football is fine in theory. The idea that the complete foot-baller can be equally comfortable in any position sounds perfect. But it does not take into account the fact that people are different. Some are tall, some are brave, some are strong; some are fat, some are slow, some are cowards. And a football team is made up of all sorts. Being a good defender, having creative vision and being a good goal-scorer are not interchangeable qualities.

DANNY BLANCHFLOWER.

At half-time I said that Dave [Mackay] and I should mark the wingers because in a true sense they were playing like inside-forwards. Our full-backs should come inside and deal with the inside-forwards. Mackay said he would prefer to mark his own man and the full-backs thought the same. I think their pride was hurt by the confusion and they each wanted to handle their own man.

DANNY BLANCHFLOWER on coping with Ipswich's new formation of deep-lying wingers under Ramsey.

Not even in the England team did I ever hear anyone tell us to go out and string some passes together. It sometimes seems that every team game in the world is about passing and possession except English football.

DOUG HOLDEN, Bolton and England winger of the **1950s**.

A pass rising a yard above the ground should be a foul. A player receiving a pass has two feet and only one head.

WILLIE READ, St Mirren manager, during his team's run to the **1959** Scottish Cup final.

I cannot stress too often my belief that people who talk of short passes and on-the-ground moves as the essence of good football do not help the progress of football in Britain.

STAN CULLIS in defence of his 'scientific kick-and-rush' Wolves, in *All for the Wolves*, **1960**.

Goal is the main objective, and theoretically all finesse which entails loss of time or ground must give way as far as possible to forging ahead.

B. O. CORBETT, Corinthians and England player, **1901**.

This long game is sheer poison because it represents a complete absence of common sense. You are asking players to whack a ball thirty or forty yards accurately under pressure. Thirty yards, which we set as a limit at Tottenham, was considered rather short. But actually it is very long.

ARTHUR ROWE, in *The Encyclopedia of Association Football*, **1960**.

Our failure has not been because we have played the English way, but because we haven't. Bloody football should be honest, open, clean, passionate. Part of a nation's culture, its heritage, is the way it plays its sport. And the English way is with passion, commitment.

GRAHAM TAYLOR, Watford manager, **1982**.

Possession, patience are myths. It is anathema to people in the game to say this, but goals come from mistakes, not possession.

GRAHAM TAYLOR.

The Watford controversy is going to become the England controversy, because that is the way we are going to be instructing at coaching courses from now on. We have worked out a formula for victory, with which it is difficult to disagree because the evidence is overwhelming.

CHARLES HUGHES, FA Chief of Coaching and advocate of the 'POMO' (Position Of Maximum Opportunity) theories of Wing-Commander Charles Reep, whose long-ball research was applied by Stan Cullis with Wolves in the **1950s**.

They are 100 years away from grasping POMO.

WING-COMMANDER REEP on managers who think the acronym simply means striking at the far post, **1984**.

$$S = \frac{R}{N \times n}$$

WING-COMMANDER REEP's equation for winning promotion, **1984**!

Did you ever, for instance, see Raich Carter running round the field as if he were being chased by all the Inner Party Members of 1984? Of course you didn't. And you didn't because Raich Carter and men like him could and did do all that the Continentals have shown us during the last few years.

NEIL FRANKLIN, former England centre-half, in *Soccer at Home and Abroad*, **1956**.

I would hope to go to a club where the players were on the same wavelength as myself and were not playing ping-pong football. There are not many players in the City side who can read my passes. Either they don't understand or they don't want to understand. Their vision is very limited. I can only help the team. I cannot make it worse.

KAZIU DENYA, Manchester City's Polish international, **1979**.

We are breeding a number of teams whose outlook seems to be that pace, punch and fitness are all that is required to win all the honours in the game. They forget that, without pure skills, these virtues count for precisely nothing.

MATT BUSBY, **1960**.

Manchester United and Spurs do have the same style, the same beliefs. Basically we believe in attack – we go out to win the game, we don't go out not to lose it.

DANNY BLANCHFLOWER, in *The Encyclopedia of Association Football*, **1960**.

You play nineteen-twentieths of the game without the ball and that's when you do your thinking. That's when you do your real playing. Any clown can play with the ball when he's got it. It's the good fellows who get into position to receive.

ARTHUR ROWE, in *The Encyclopedia of Association Football*, **1960**.

Tottenham's and United's style is based on the belief that possession of the ball is all that matters and you are better off with the ball in your own penalty box than to have it in the opposition's penalty box with two players fighting for it.

ARTHUR ROWE, as above.

Balloon ball. The percentage game. Route one. . .It's crept into the First Division. We get asked to lend youngsters to these teams. We won't do it. They come back with bad habits, big legs and good eyesight.

RON ATKINSON, Manchester United manager, on the long-ball game, **1984**.

When a man starts to run with the ball, the only man who can possibly know what he is going to do is the chap who is running with it. And nine times out of ten even he doesn't know.

ARTHUR ROWE, in *The Encyclopedia of Association Football*, **1960**.

It took me sixteen years to realize that this is a passing, not a dribbling, game.

JIMMY HILL, television presenter and former Fulham forward, **1970s**.

We have learned to bawl 'Get rid of it' just as the mob in the French Revolution bawled 'To the Guillotine'. And our get-rid-of-it addicts successfully sent our soccer to the sporting guillotine.

NEIL FRANKLIN, former England defender, in *Soccer at Home and Abroad*, **1956**.

Never try to whitewash British football by saying that the Continentals would not live in the First Division. They wouldn't want to. They prefer to play their football under conditions which allow the game to be played properly.

NEIL FRANKLIN, as above.

If you don't start belting that ball out of the penalty area, I'll get some big ignorant lad who can do the job better.

BRIAN CLOUGH to defenders Todd, Nish and McFarland at Birmingham *v*. Derby match, **1973**.

No footballer of talent should play in the back four.

MALCOLM ALLISON, **1975**.

The attitude in England is tricks are okay if they work. . .if they don't you're a wanker. It doesn't seem to have sunk in that if you never try you'll never succeed.

DUNCAN McKENZIE, **1976**.

Recently I went home to England and saw Forest play Villa with twenty players crowded into a third of the pitch, and I wondered, 'Did I really play this kind of football?'

TONY WOODCOCK, Cologne and England striker, **1980**.

It is no surprise that England are suffering a list of injuries, because of the impossible strain you impose on them by playing too much football. There is a marked decline between October and April in the performance of your players, and you cannot underestimate the psychological effect of recent club defeats in Cup semi-finals and finals. Such blows to the nervous system take weeks to heal. You are plagued with 'industrial football', yet the potential you have remains enormous.

MILJAN MILJANIC, Yugoslav manager of Real Madrid, **1976**.

In the last twelve months, going round to League matches, it has been increasingly obvious that skills do not have the chance to develop because of the fierce physical contact.

DON REVIE, a year after leaving Leeds United to manage England, **1975**.

As soon as it dawned on me that we were short of players who combined skill and commitment, I should have forgotten all about trying to play more controlled, attractive football, and settled for a real bastard of a team.

REVIE after his resignation as England manager, **1977**.

Brazil don't expect Zico to tackle back. It might be worth taking a chance on a midfield player whose principal asset is not his lungs.

PETER SHREEVE, Spurs coach, in defence of Glenn Hoddle, **1982**.

With only three defenders it was different. The back on the far side was always covering behind the centre-half so the winger always had space from the crossfield pass. With four defenders the backs can play tight on the winger and he's lost his acceleration space. Without that a winger's finished. He's just got to keep looking for an opening. So it's better to opt for work-rate, for a player who will go again, show his courage and not be confined to the touch-line.

DAVE BOWEN, Wales manager, in Tony Pawson, *The Football Managers*, **1973**.

Unlike the Brazilians we start looking for faults as soon as we recognize a player's skill. I've had it pushed down my throat ever since I was a kid. Of course the runners and tacklers are part of the game, but people don't have a go at them if they can't play forty-yard balls or go past three men at a time. They don't expect them to do the things skilful players are good at. . . .That is the way we are in England and maybe it's part of the reason Brazil do a bit more than us at international level.

GLENN HODDLE, Spurs and England midfield player, **1981**.

I admire English football. Your players have everything that is necessary to be successful. But you don't always use all the possibilities. Maybe an outsider could introduce a more effective system.

SEPP PIONTEK, German-born manager of Denmark, **1983**.

Football is a physical game. It's about stamina and strength and players battling for each other. A lot of people knock those qualities – but that's what English football is all about.

RON SAUNDERS, Aston Villa manager, on the way to the League title in **1981**.

Northern Ireland and Wales have their success partly because they take the attitude they are only going to survive if they are together and give it the gun. . .Playing together as a team hides a lot of evils.

STEVE PERRYMAN in *A Man For All Seasons*, **1985**.

'Whatever else may come down or off, you must have shorts! And there is nothing quite so likely to put you off the fine edge of your game as any kind of uncertainty about them.' *FA Book for Boys 1951-52*

Rule 3: Kicks must be aimed only at the ball

'The thing I envy about Celtic and Rangers is the loyalty they get from their players. They're not interested in playing for anyone else.' Harry Catterick, Everton manager, 1964. *Above,* Celtic-style commitment 1980

'You've beaten them once. Now go out and bloody beat them again.' Alf Ramsey to England team before extra time in 1966 World Cup final

'Souness kicked me . . . I always seem to have trouble from him.' Terry Yorath after Wales *v.* Scotland 1979. *Above,* Yorath tackles Souness during that match

'No, signor, it is not dancing school.' Claudio Gentile of Italy on his rough treatment of Diego Maradona in the Italy-Argentina World Cup match, 1982

'God's judgement willed that luck fell on the German side.' Chancellor Schmidt on West Germany's win over France in 1982. *Below,* Schumacher's notorious collision with Battiston: luck willed that the German keeper was not sent off

'Isn't one of the main features of football-match attendance still that it enables men to get away from nagging wives?' Frank Burrows, Portsmouth manager, 1981

'To have Alf Ramsey as my vice-captain was always a source of inspiration . . . His whole being is centred upon playing good football to beat the opposition.' Billy Wright, 1959. *Below*, Alf Ramsey in action for Spurs in 1953

'It took me sixteen years to realize that this is a passing, not a dribbling, game.' Jimmy Hill, seen below playing for Fulham

Team spirit is an illusion that you only glimpse when you win.

STEVE ARCHIBALD, Barcelona, Scotland and former Spurs striker, **1985**.

The enemies of football argue that the game rouses the combative instinct in one; the friends reply that therefore there is all the more reason why the game should be played, because a golden attribute is the quality of curbing one's temper, and long experience of football tends to this.

JOHN GOODALL, a member of Preston North End's double-winning team, **1889**.

I'm not here to play fitba', I'm here to see you don't play fitba'.

SCOTTISH CENTRE-HALF to R. S. McColl of Rangers and Scotland, in the **1890s**.

It was more rugged [in the 1930s and 1940s]. There was more physical contact. We always had what we called the killers in the game, players who went deliberately over the ball to get the man. They were all known, and you took special precautions against them. The play was rougher and dirtier than it is now.

STAN CULLIS, ex-Wolves captain and manager, in Arthur Hopcraft, *The Football Man*, **1968**.

In the Northern section of the Third Division there is a harsh accent in the football. It is against the Northern teams of this rank that the highest caste Southern teams fear to play in Cup ties. From the Southern section this harshness is often absent. It is not that the football is better – for far too much is aerial – but more suave.

DR PERCY M. YOUNG in *Football Year*, **1956**.

The older principles whereby success was hacked out from rival limbs are now discredited in the best circles.

DR PERCY M. YOUNG in *Football Year*, **1956**.

English football has degenerated to unbelievable levels. The hackers are now completely in charge.

JOHNNY BYRNE, ex-West Ham and England player, **1973**.

I'm no angel, but I've never kicked anyone deliberately.

BILLY BREMNER, **1967**.

Next thing we'll be giving our handbags to the linesmen as we skip onto the field.

MIKE SUMMERBEE, Manchester City forward, on referees' clampdown of **1971**.

I've got more points than Man United.

MIKE SUMMERBEE.

Angels don't win you anything except a place in heaven – football teams need one or two vagabonds.

BILLY McNEILL, Manchester City manager, **1983**.

Bad behaviour off the field is seldom a product of bad behaviour on the field. In fact there is much less thuggery in football today than there was when I was starting out thirty years ago.

BOBBY ROBSON in *Time on the Grass*, **1982**.

I apologized afterwards to Roberts. He's a hard man himself and understands these things. I'm sure he'll get his own back over the next five years.

ANDY GRAY, Wolves striker, after injuring Spurs' Graham Roberts, **1983**.

I have people in custody for doing less than the Spurs players did to Fulham on Wednesday.

FULHAM POLICE INSPECTOR after Spurs *v*. Fulham FA Cup replay, **1984**.

Never had a ball. Oranges. All the time oranges.

KENNY ACHAMPONG, Fulham winger, on how he acquired his ball control, **1985**.

I have not seen much of English football, but it seems as if it always has a lot of high balls, strong marking and strong running. Of course, in England, football is played on the pitches of winter. It should be played in summer. In Brazil we play more or less all the year round and on some very dry and very bad pitches. But it produces some very good players.

CARLOS ALBERTO, Brazil's 1970 World Cup-winning captain, in **1983** as coach to world club champions Flamengo.

Our football comes from the heart, theirs comes from the mind.

PELE on the difference between South American and European soccer, **1970**.

These are players; men who play with their heads and their hearts.

FERENC PUSKAS.

A footballer is someone who can make his feet obey his head.

TIBOR NYILASI, Hungary captain, **1985**.

We cling to the myth that our Football League is the best in the world. There are others: the West German and South American Leagues for example are as good. But it *is* the toughest in its demands on players and it *is* destructive of national football in its drain of players' energy and in denying them time for national commitments.

SIR STANLEY ROUS in *Football Worlds – a Lifetime in Sport*, **1978**.

Other countries have their history. Uruguay has its football.

ONDINA VIERA, Uruguay manager in **1966**.

This is the worst football we have ever played. It is a national disgrace; we shall be publicly tried on our return.

URUGUAY MANAGER in **1974** World Cup.

Dutch football at the moment is at the crossroads. Their best football compares with that of teams like Walthamstow Avenue, Romford, Leytonstone, Bishop Auckland and Crook Town. . . . The sooner professionalism comes to Dutch football, the better it will be.

TOMMY LAWTON, former England centre-forward, in *Soccer the Lawton Way*, **1954**. Within twenty years Holland had reached the World Cup final.

I don't go much for this hugging and kissing in soccer – that's one Continental idea we'll never bring to Upton Park. . . . Another thing I don't like is this Continental insistence on not charging the goalkeeper. Why not? Why should he have immunity?

TED FENTON, West Ham manager, in *At Home with the Hammers*, **1960**.

England's idea of choosing the best eleven players from a number of clubs and expecting them to play together as a team is out of date. It was all right so long as players stuck rigidly to their positions on the field, but that system is no longer effective in modern football.

FERENC PUSKAS, after Hungary's 7–1 over England in Budapest, 1954, in *Captain of Hungary*, **1955**.

Throughout the game we demonstrated the golden rule of modern football; and that is: the good player keeps playing even without the ball. All the time he is placing himself so that when the ball comes to him he is able to make good use of it. We improved the English saying 'Kick and run' to 'Pass accurately and run into a good position.'

PUSKAS on Hungary's 6–3 defeat of England at Wembley in **1953**.

When I returned to the Cumberland Hotel, a small boy came up to me in the foyer and said: 'Please sir, take me to your country and teach me to play football.'

PUSKAS in *Captain of Hungary*, **1955**.

Perhaps England, once the masters, can now learn from the pupils.

PUSKAS, after Hungary's 1953 win at Wembley.

We have nothing to learn from these people.

SIR ALF RAMSEY after defeat by Brazil, 1970.

The Continentals hold that ball, pass it back, sideways, frontways, any way, to deprive the opposition from getting it. We must bring some of their artistry into our more direct game.

DON REVIE in *Soccer's Happy Wanderer*, 1956.

Good Continental teams will play football right from their own goalmouth, whereas most teams in the Football League desperately strive to get the ball as far as the halfway line before worrying about a constructive move. Who would deny that we are now not primarily concerned so much about playing football as about preventing the opposition from playing it?

MATT BUSBY in *My Story*, 1957.

Brazil played in shoes which could only be likened to Grecian slippers. We cannot laugh even about that. After all, they won the World Cup in them.

TOM FINNEY on the 1958 World Cup in *Finney on Football*, 1958.

I have yet to see a great football team made up of ninety-minute triers. The 1954 Hungarians, the 1958 Brazilians, and the brilliant club teams like Real Madrid, included many players who would be damned in English eyes for disappearing for spells during a game. Puskas, Pele, Didi and Garrincha all do it, yet each has sufficient skills to win a match in ten minutes, or less.

JIMMY McILROY, Burnley and Northern Ireland midfield player, in *Right Inside Soccer*, 1960.

The Continentals fundamentally are far more artistic; it pleases them better to exploit the art and craft of football rather than brute force and strength.

ARTHUR ROWE, in *The Encyclopedia of Association Football*, **1960**.

Italian League football was rubbish – totally defensive. Games were either no score, or 1–0. Rarely were more than two goals scored. When we had lost a couple of matches, we began to feel the attitude of the directors. It was as though we had lost a war. Too important! With a reaction like that, players don't want to be adventurous.

DENIS LAW on his spell with Torino in the early 1960s in *An Autobiography*, **1979**.

The game [in Italy] was like life and death for everybody: for the players, for the directors, for everybody. That can't be the right way. It was not enjoyable to play, and surely not enjoyable to watch, and yet the grounds were always full: which says something about how important the game was to a lot of Italian people. Football was their whole life.

DENIS LAW, as above.

If a team out here (Italy) made that sort of start I don't think the players would dare be seen on the streets – they'd be condemned to hide in their houses.

TREVOR FRANCIS of Sampdoria on West Brom's long losing run, **1985**.

My summing-up of Continental football is that they are marvellous winners but damn bad losers. Their acts of sportsmanship are insincere; they play a scientific style of football, it's true, but when we employ similar methods they resort to unfair tactics. We taught them how to play football, but they have manufactured unsporting actions of their own.

BOB LORD, Burnley chairman, in *My Fight for Football*, **1963**.

I may shock people when I say I haven't any real desire to turn out in European Cup matches, even though the entire population of Burnley awaits these matches with tremendous enthusiasm in the season ahead. A wonderful tournament when it started, it has degenerated into a succession of rough-house games all over the Continent. Rough-house tactics are all right for boxers or wrestlers, but I have always been taught that footballers should be more concerned with artistry.

JIMMY McILROY, Burnley and Northern Ireland midfield player, in *Right Inside Soccer*, **1960**.

You moan about the European Cup. You curse the hotels, raise hell about the training pitches, lug your own food about, worry about the referees, about the injuries, about the air strikes, the heating in the player's rooms, the travel weariness. . .and then the moment you are out of it, you are empty inside. The icing is off the cake. God, you do miss it.

BOB PAISLEY.

We went to Porto and there was a bloody hurricane. We come here (Rome) and the shops are shut. When we play in Russia, Reagan will probably have the place blown up.

JIM STEEL, Wrexham striker, during club's European run, **1984**.

Our attitude to the European Cup was comparable to our later approach to the European Common Market. We would have been better off if we had gone in sooner.

ROY SWINBOURNE, Wolves centre-forward of the 1950s, in Motson and Rowlinson, *The European Cup 1955–80*, **1980**.

Frankly, some of the organization in the early stages of the European Cup smacked of a chip shop approach.

ARTHUR ELLIS, Halifax referee, in Motson and Rowlinson, *The European Cup 1955–80*, **1980**.

There is no limit to what this team can achieve. We will win the European Cup. European football is full of cowards and we will terrorize them with our power and attacking football.

MALCOLM ALLISON after Manchester City's **1968** League championship. City lost to Fenerbahce (Turkey) in the first round in 1968–69.

When I saw the most honoured club team in Europe chopping [John] Charles down so brutally, I realized the convictions I had about the European Cup, when I was refereeing in it myself, were being proved correct. The competition was getting out of hand. The will to win had become the predominant factor and the financial incentives for the players were almost making it a matter of life and death.

ARTHUR ELLIS after watching Juventus v. Real Madrid on television in **1962**. In *The European Cup 1955–80*.

I told him he had no need to stoop to that with his sort of skill.

RON GREENWOOD, then Chelsea centre-half, on being badly fouled by Hidegkuti, Hungary's centre-forward, Chelsea v. Red Banner, **1954**.

The Continentals shudder when they think of how football is played in Britain. . . . What horrifies them is the British love of bodily contact, and it is doubtful whether any Italian player would last a season of hard, rugged British tackling.

JOHN CHARLES after leaving Leeds for Juventus, in *The Gentle Giant*, **1962**.

When you come to a place like Barcelona you think 'Bloody Hell, I wish I was back in England.'

TERRY BUTCHER, Ipswich defender, **1979**.

The organizing committee, in its wisdom, allocated the 1954 World Cup to Switzerland, where the locals appear to be more interested in climbing up and down their mountains, explaining why their clocks and watches are so much better than any others in the world, or generally catering for their annual influx of non-football tourists. Four years later, Sweden is honoured, and I *cannot* imagine why.

TOM FINNEY in *Finney on Football*, **1958**.

We have still to produce our best football. It will come against a team who come to play football and not act as animals.

ALF RAMSEY after England's brawl with Argentina, **1966** World Cup.

It looks as though brutality pays. Running with the ball, I found as never before that my calculations were disturbed not by fears of a hard, legal tackle, for that is in the game, but by thoughts that I had certain opponents whose chief aim was to disable me.

PELE on **1966** World Cup, in *My Life and the Beautiful Game*, **1977**.

Morais of Portugal had a field day fouling me, and eventually putting me out of the game. He tripped me and, when I was stumbling to the ground, he leapt at me, feet first, and cut me down completely. It wasn't until I actually saw the films of the game that I realized what a terribly vicious double-foul it was. . . . The English referee allowed Morais to remain on the field, although again, in the most inexperienced league in the world he would have been thrown out for either of the fouls, let alone both.

PELE on the end of his and Brazil's World Cup, 1966, in *My Life and the Beautiful Game*, **1977**.

I have heard it said since, and firmly believe it, that Sir Stanley Rous, the British president of FIFA at the time who selected the referees at Liverpool where the game was played, had instructed the referees to go easy on the 'virile' game played by European teams against the South Americans, with the result that Zhechev (Bulgaria) did everything he could to physically cripple me, and the referee, Jim Finney, gave neither me nor any of the others on our team the protection we had a right to expect.

PELE on 1966 World Cup in *My Life and the Beautiful Game*, **1977**.

The English side was granted privileges by Rous while all kinds of obstacles were created for its most dangerous rivals such as biased refereeing, and inconvenient schedules for matches and training sessions.

TASS (Official Soviet News Agency) on role of the 'notorious' Sir Stanley Rous (then FIFA president) in England's **1966** World Cup victory.

There was a band this mornin', playin' outside our hotel at five o'clock in the mornin'. We were promised a police escort to the ground; it never arrived. When my players went out onto the pitch, they were abused and jeered by the crowd. I would have thought that the Mexican public would have been delighted to welcome England. Then, when the game began, they could cheer their own team as much as they liked. But we are delighted to be in Mexico, and the Mexican people are a wonderful people.

SIR ALF RAMSEY to Mexican press in Azteca Stadium, World Cup **1970**.

Every English player autographed my leg with his studs.

GUNTHER NETZER of West Germany after bitter 0–0 draw in the European Championships qualifying round in **1972**.

Football is not played at top level by a bunch of charity-minded nuns, but the Argentinians are no more dirty or less sporting than anyone else. In any case there are two sides to every coin and if English players or fans think that the Argentinians are dirty players I can assure you that the Argentinians feel exactly the same. Everyone in Buenos Aires is firmly convinced that the dirtiest players they ever saw came from England.

ALFREDO DI STEFANO, ex-Real Madrid, Argentina and Spain, **1973**.

It [Scottish approach to football] stems from a great conceit or, perhaps, a myth, that in Scottish football there is an inspired, spontaneous geometry of purest origin which, when it comes right, will benefit even the defeated. For they could learn from the vision of perfection, a perfection that is of people, made by people, by wee, bitter, narrow, ill-educated men yet full of light and luminous grace.

JOHN RAFFERTY, soccer journalist, in *One Hundred Years of Scottish Football*, **1973**.

Still the Scottish football ground is the place to go when you're half pissed, to urinate down the back of the man in front of you and to use the language of the barrack room. And, among two legions of supporters in this country, the place to go to sing those hateful songs of Ireland.

IAN ARCHER, soccer journalist, in *When Will We See Your Like Again?*, **1977**.

If Scotland ever discover that football is a team game, the rest of us will have to watch out.

JOHN ADAMS, FA Northern Region staff coach, **1980s**.

They're not so different. They've got two arms and two legs and some of them even have heads.

FRANK 'MAD DOG' AROK, Australian manager, on Scotland team before World Cup tie at Hampden, **1985**.

We didn't even have Scotland track suits. We had to bring our own training gear. And what a peculiar lot we looked among the world's best, with the green of Celtic and the white of Preston and the blue of Dundee contrasting with the beautifully turned out teams of Europe and South America. We looked like liquorice allsorts.

WILLIE FERNIE, Celtic and Scotland player, on Scotland's first, disastrous World Cup in 1954, in *When Will We See Your Like Again?*, **1977**.

We were nearly fainting in the heat. But all the advice we remember getting was voices from the touchline commanding: 'Get stuck into it.'

NEILLY MOCHAN, Celtic and Scotland player, on Uruguay 7, Scotland 0, 1954 World Cup, as above.

Prestige is precious to a little trading nation and there is no quicker way to earn it than through football.

JOHN RAFFERTY, *The Scotsman*, **1971**.

It is difficult to stay in an unhealthy house without catching some of the disease.

JOCK STEIN, then manager of Celtic, on Scottish football. *When Will We See Your Like Again?*, **1977**.

The Scots are a hard team, and play with excessive violence.

ZAGALO, Brazil manager, on hearing World Cup draw, **1974**.

We were provoked by England being so good. This is modern football. We must be up to date.

CLAUDIO COUTINHO, Brazil manager, after rough match with England, **1978**.

We were bombarded with crap about beating the rest of the world into the ground. How could anyone be so optimistic about our chances? When did you last see a Scotland team play really good football, play with positive rhythm and a consistent pattern? It was a fight when we beat the Czechs and a fight when we beat the Welsh at Anfield. Tunisia and Iran are better prepared than we are. In our last match before coming here the lads exhausted themselves trying to beat England. It couldn't be any other way with 80,000 mad Scotsmen yelling, 'Gie us an English heid.'

LOU MACARI in Argentina with the Scotland team under Ally MacLeod, **1978**.

I am proud of my team for beating the best side in Europe. I want to congratulate Scotland for the team they presented to us.

MARCUS CALDERON, Peru manager, during **1978** World Cup.

The World Cups of 1958 and 1962 were garden parties compared with what is involved now, with the pressures that have developed. The increase in pressure seems continuous from one competition to the next. In 1966 it was already terrific, in 1970 it was worse, in 1974 still more terrible and now it is almost completely out of hand. Football has become almost a kind of war.

HELMUT SCHOEN, West Germany manager, during **1978** World Cup.

Football became popular because it was considered an art, but now too many pitches are becoming battlefields.

SOCRATES, Brazil captain, **1981**.

The tackling in international football is frightening. Even a nation like the Swiss, not noted for ruthlessness, have joined in.

GEOFF HURST, assistant to England manager Ron Greenwood, **1981**.

No, signor, it is not dancing school.

CLAUDIO GENTILE of Italy on his rough treatment of Diego Maradona in the Italy-Argentina World Cup match, **1982**.

We need someone to play dirty at times. We missed a player like that in the 1982 finals. Italy, for example, had Gentile, who had no pity when he wanted to hit an opponent.

ZICO, Brazilian midfield player, **1986**.

It was beautifully done. It was wrong, but it was necessary.

JACK CHARLTON commentating on a 'professional foul' in Barcelona v. Dusseldorf game, **1979**.

There's more experts in this game than any other sport I've ever seen.

JOHN ROONEY, owner of the Philadelphia Spartans, **1967**.

I don't even know what a soccer ball looks like.

DICK WALSH on being appointed Commissioner of the United States Soccer Association, the precursor of the North American Soccer League (NASL), **1967**.

If the US becomes enthralled by soccer it will be when every back street and stretch of urban waste ground has its teams of kids playing their makeshift matches, the players claiming the temporary identity of the world's stars in the sport. Environments like that produce those stars. Football is an inner compulsion. It cannot be settled on a people like instant coffee.

ARTHUR HOPCRAFT, *The Football Man*, **1968**.

Those Stoker guys are so cocky they make me mad saying ours is a dull game. Boy, if ours is dull, theirs is even duller. Those nuts. Running around in shorts, chasing a big ball like a bunch of schoolboys.

JOE AZCUE, Cleveland Indians baseball coach, **1967**. Cleveland Stokers were Stoke City.•

Soccer is a game in which everyone does a lot of running around. . . . Mostly, twenty-one guys stand around and one guy does a tap dance with the ball. It's about as exciting as *Tristan and Isolde*.

JIM MURRAY, *Louisville Courier Journal*, **1967**.

Where are we going? What the hell are we doing? Why the hell do these people keep paying me?

ALKIS PANAGOULIAS, USA national coach, on state of soccer in his country before 5–0 defeat by England, **1985**.

To say that American soccer is the football of the future is ludicrous. You've got to see football in the black townships of South Africa or Rio before you can talk about the football of the future. I read a lot about American soccer and I still can't name five top American players.

JACK TAYLOR, English World Cup referee, **1978**.

America is the land of opportunity for soccer.

RON NEWMAN, Fort Lauderdale Striker's coach, **1978**.

It's an elephant's graveyard.

GIANNI RIVERA, Milan and Italy, on rejecting an offer from the USA, **1978**.

Because in this bloody country, Americans think that any guy who runs around in shorts kicking a ball instead of catching it has to be a Commie or a fairy.

CLIVE TOYE, New York Cosmos' British general manager, on why the club gave away so many 'promos' and 'freebies', **1970**.

In England, soccer is a grey game played by grey people on grey days.

RODNEY MARSH, to Florida television audience, **1979**.

With such refinements as a thirty-five-yard offside law, synthetic pitches which are not conducive to tackling, 'shoot-outs' to eliminate drawn games and bonus points, the country which gave the world Disneyland has provided a Mickey Mouse football industry.

JACK ROLLIN on the NASL in *Rothman's Football Yearbook* **1979–80**.

Tell the Kraut to get his ass up front. We don't pay a million for a guy to hang around in defense.

NEW YORK COSMOS executive on Franz Beckenbauer's tendency to play deep.

The indoor game definitely provides more what the American fan wants to see. The outdoor game is better, there's more strategy and tactics. But in America they like a winner and they like action. It's like the ice hockey – I went to a game which was more like a fight and that's what the crowd love. They like the physical stuff.

KEITH WELLER, ex-England player with Fort Lauderdale Strikers, **1983**.

People think it's a soft touch in the North American Soccer League but it's hard out there, I can tell you. You travel from one side of the continent to the other, play the next day, fly back and play two days later. You have astroturf and grass and 90° heat with 95° humidity, all these things to contend with. So you can't get away with sitting on the beach and drinking.

KEITH WELLER, **1983**.

If you can't hit a thirty-yard ball to feet here, you won't be able to do it anywhere.

JIMMY GREAVES on QPR's Omniturf, before the first League match on it, **1981**.

It was a nightmare. Forwards can turn you early, you daren't commit yourself. I can't see many teams getting a point here.

TERRY BOYLE, Crystal Palace reserves defender, after first-ever competitive match on QPR's artificial surface, **1981**.

They tell me that pitch is where the game's future lies. If that's so, I'm glad I'm getting on a bit. . . . But I was delighted to get a point. Normally the only thing we get out of London is the train from Euston.

JIMMY FRIZZELL, Oldham manager, on the Omniturf, **1981**.

Scientists are hinting that Northern Europe may be entering a new Ice Age.

QPR programme editorial extolling virtues of artificial pitches during bitter winter, **1986**.

It's an old stable. Players wash-up in a horse trough. The pitch is a bog, cramped and small. The team play 5–4–1 and that's when they are feeling adventurous. [It's] the sort of place that makes you wonder what you ever saw in football. If the walls of that cupboard they call a dressing-room could talk, they'd spend the first month reeling off the names of those who had lost there and given up the game forever.

TIVIDALE PLAYER'S description of West Midland League rivals Hednesford's ground in Brian James, *Journey to Wembley*, **1977**.

Teams hate coming to The Den. I remember going there with York City for my first visit. It took us half an hour to find the place. Eventually we went up this dingy back street. I remember thinking, 'Where is this?' Then you go and have a look at the pitch, which is bumpy, terrible. The away team dressing-room is a dungeon, no light, no window. The bathrooms are horrible. Then you get out there to face them – the Lions. And they come storming at you and most sides jack it in. . . . When you have been there a little time, though, you grow to love it. It's one of our biggest assets.

EAMON DUNPHY in *Only a Game?*, **1976**.

They did well to get a point. Usually all teams get at Millwall is the tyres let down on their coaches.

TOMMY DOCHERTY on a team earning a draw at The Den, **1985**.

It's the only stadium in the world I've ever been in that's absolutely buzzing with atmosphere when it's empty and there isn't a soul inside. It's almost like a cathedral.

TOMMY DOCHERTY on Old Trafford, in *Call the Doc*, **1982**.

Blimey, the ground looks a bit different to Watford. Where's the dog track?

LUTHER BLISSETT at Milan's San Siro Stadium, **1983**.

I cordially agree with his [Goodall's] views about all the excessive training of modern days and I am sure that the game has greatly deteriorated and that skill and manoeuvres have given place to pace and speed.

G. O. SMITH on John Goodall's death in the 1940s, in Edward Grayson, *Corinthians, Casuals and Cricketers*, **1955**.

At present the players stand about six yards away from the goalkeeper and shoot, which any navvy could do. There is no running about or dribbling, feinting, passing with the inside or outside of the foot, trapping or heading the ball and placing it with the head like you do with your feet, judging distances etc, indulged in at all. Players should, in my opinion, try to do the things with the ball they have to do on a Saturday.

CHARLIE ROBERTS, Manchester United captain, in the *Football Players' Magazine*, **1913**.

If you are playing a match for an hour and a half on Saturday you shouldn't spend two hours a day training. You don't want to leave all your vitality on the training track.

DANNY BLANCHFLOWER in *The Encyclopedia of Association Football*, **1960**.

Another feature of England training is 'mime-practice'. As you jog round, you go through all the motions without a ball that you do when you have the ball. You trap, pass, volley, head for goal, head clear and weight imaginary passes. All that is missing is the ball.

PHIL NEAL, Liverpool and England right-back, in *Attack From The Back*, **1981**.

The hardest thing was to get them to go out. . .to improve on the weaknesses in their game. There seemed to be a latent resentment or shyness to try to do something they couldn't in case their team-mates laughed at them. They would sooner reserve it for a Saturday afternoon and show 50,000 spectators that they couldn't do it.

ARTHUR ROWE on players in the 1950s, in *The Encyclopedia of Association Football*, **1960**.

I always wore ordinary brown boots at football with a more or less pointed toe and very thin stockings. To my mind it is difficult to make delicate passes and to shoot with the rather clumsy square-toed boots that professionals use.

G.O. SMITH, Corinthians and England player, in Edward Grayson, *Corinthians, Casuals and Cricketers*, **1955**.

Each man uses only his own kit. As soon as he takes it off, sweater, track suit, jersey, whatever it may be the item is dropped into a pile of other dirty clothing and taken away for washing. There is no chance of the 'itch' going through our dressing-room. . . .

TOM WHITTAKER, former Arsenal manager, in *Tom Whittaker's Arsenal Story*, **1958**.

Whatever else may come down or off, you must have shorts! And there is nothing quite so likely to put you off the fine edge of your game as any kind of uncertainty about them. Who hasn't had that nightmare of finding himself without trousers? Your good pair of shorts ought to have a pocket of some kind, somewhere. You may go to a match in a jacket in which you can risk leaving your bus-fare or even a toffee, but there is one thing you should have during a game – a handkerchief. You may need this for blowing your nose, or you may need it for getting dirt out of your eye or wiping away the manly sweat from your brow – or even blood from a wound! It is remarkable how education authorities go for elaborate lessons in hygiene and then supply school teams with shorts that have no pocket. Do they think footballers should blow their noses on their sleeves?

REV. PAUL GEDGE, 'You and Your Playing Kit', in *FA Book For Boys*, **1951–52**.

Every hour of the day he lives in an atmosphere which reminds
him of nothing else but football; and he finishes the week by
playing before a great crowd of people, who often expect him to
perform more like a machine than a human being subject to pains,
aches and illnesses, to say nothing of the ugly wound which the
stud of a boot has opened, but which his pluck and loyalty to his
club causes him to forget in his whole-souled desire to secure a
victory for his side.

WILLIAM (BILLY) MEREDITH in *Association Football and the Men Who Made It*,
1906.

Even for a player who is stable and experienced there can be
murderous pressure. One match that I played in. . .will live with
me always. For three or four hours before the game I experienced
a marvellous sense of anticipation. . . . Then, as we kicked about
before the start, I felt the strength drain away from me. It took
a great effort to put one foot in front of the other. My legs felt
rubbery. I wondered if I was going to faint.

MALCOLM ALLISON on the Spurs *v.* West Ham, FA Cup sixth round tie, 1956, in
Colours of My Life, **1975**.

The game almost broke the health of a highly intelligent man like
Joe Mercer. It cut George Best off at adolescence. It has the
power to destroy because it releases unnatural forces. It creates
an unreal atmosphere of excitement and it deals in elation and
despair and it bestows these emotions at least once a week.

MALCOLM ALLISON, as above.

As a player it's like living in a box. Someone takes you out of the
box for training and the games. . .and makes all the decision for
you. I have seen players – famous internationals – in an airport
lounge all get up and follow one bloke into the lav. Six of them,
maybe, standing there not wanting to piss themselves, but
following the bloke who does. Like sheep. . .because that's the
way they've been trained: to sit, stand, follow the bloke in front,
never asking why. It's daft, but it's the system.

GEOFF HURST, in Brian James, *Journey to Wembley*, **1977**.

The mystery that was in my mind
is sinking slow
And my hands that once were frozen
are thawing fast:–
Its shame on me that my day

has been long coming,
But yet its been so hard for me
to gauge the proper distance:–
The velvet touch that now is close
within my grasp
Is indeed most well befitting
to your chimes of glory:–

JOHN FARMER, from his poem, 'For Gordon Banks'.

A day is a long time in football. The last result, that is all. If
Palace win on Saturday they will feel great. Now if you had asked
them at the beginning of the season how they would feel if they
were seven points adrift at the bottom and they won a game
making it five points adrift, they would have been speechless.
Probably not able to envisage how awful they would feel. But if
they win on Saturday they will feel great. One win and you are
away. The dream is on again and off you go.

EAMON DUNPHY, in *Only a Game?*, **1976**.

I get on the team bus these days and the back seat is always
empty. You used to be in the side for a few years before they'd
let you anywhere near the back seat. Now the young lads are all
doing *The Times* crossword or playing Scrabble. I'm not saying
that's so bad but I find it all a bit hard to take.

ALAN BALL, **1982**.

If he is married he has to say goodbye to many of the pleasures
of home life, and at the festive time of year, when everyone
reckons to meet round the family circle, he is probably hundreds
of miles away, perhaps shut up in a deserted seaside resort, under-
going 'special training' for the purpose of providing entertainment
for the more favoured members of society. Add to all this the
possible risk of having to stay for weeks in hospital nursing a

broken ankle or a dislocated collar bone, and it must surely be agreed that the life of the professional football player is not quite so gilded an occupation as it might appear.

WILLIAM (BILLY) MEREDITH in *Association Football and the Men Who Made It*, **1906**.

Before us was the kind of scene we had conjured up in our minds after seeing numerous Hollywood travel films, and such productions as *Flying Down to Rio* with Fred Astaire and 'Ginger' Rogers, but when team manager Walter Winterbottom informed us that the beach was out of bounds I felt I might as well be in my own back garden in Tettenhall as in this South American paradise.

BILLY WRIGHT on the Copacabana Beach, Rio de Janeiro, before the 1950 World Cup, in *Captain of England*, **1950**.

Before a match I take out my false teeth, and stick them in my cap which I keep in the back of the net. It's a habit I have adopted in important matches, just in case I have to meet someone at short notice or at the end of a game. Then I can always pop my teeth in.

RONNIE SIMPSON, Celtic goalkeeper, in *Sure It's a Grand Old Team to Play For*, **1967**.

'Man, I'm glad that I'm doing this course in the afternoons. This footballer's life of training in the morning and walking round the Manchester shops in the afternoon is so boring.'
  'Oh, me and my mate don't just walk round the Manchester shops. Sometimes we go to Wilmslow instead.'

EXCHANGE between two Manchester-based players on an England Under-21 meeting.

I prefer players not to be too good or clever at other things. It means they concentrate on football.

BILL NICHOLSON, Spurs manager, **1973**.

What they say about footballers being ignorant is rubbish. I spoke to a couple yesterday and they were quite intelligent.

RAQUEL WELCH, after visit to Chelsea match, **1973**.

Some say that professional players should study, or learn another profession, so that they can do something else after they quit football. That is unrealistic, if not impossible. If I have to prepare myself mentally and physically for every game, how can I sit with a book in my hands studying until an hour before kick-off? If I'm going to play well I have to concentrate and build myself up for the match. I think this failure to understand the physical and mental strains on a professional is behind the widely held belief that footballers are stupid.

JOHAN CRUYFF, then an Ajax player, in **1973**.

We have left nothing to chance. The players do not have to swallow a crumb of Russian food if they so wish. We are travelling with a full kitchen of Irish food – rashers, eggs, black pudding, steaks, ketchup. There can be no excuses on this score.

FA OF IRELAND OFFICIAL on the Republic's preparations for a match in the Soviet Union, **1985**.

The stomach plays a very important part in footer, and lets a chap down badly if it is not in the right condition on the day of the match. In my youth I always had a big meal an hour or so before the game. That is wrong. The general procedure is a good breakfast and a very light lunch – consisting of boiled mutton, or fish, or – what I consider best – a poached egg on well-crisped toast. If this is carried out faithfully a great improvement will be noticed regarding wind, and you'll find you will be able to last out a hard encounter much easier.

EDDIE HAPGOOD, Arsenal and England full-back, on 'Faults to Avoid in Soccer', in *Boy's Own Paper*, **1939**.

I have never known a group of people like footballers for eating.
A huge evening meal is digested and forgotten by 9.30pm. Then
they still want endless rounds of sandwiches.

ALEC STOCK in *A Little Thing Called Pride*, **1982**.

I saw him on one occasion shift two steak pies, a heaped plate of
potatoes and vegetables, two helpings of apple tart and literally
gallons of tea.

ROY PAUL, Manchester City and Wales player, of John Charles in *A Red Dragon
of Wales*, **1956**.

'A bit crude when eating' states the report of an Arsenal scout.
He was referring to a well-known international in whom Arsenal
were interested. The description shows how deeply the club vet
a man for whose transfer they may make a bid, and the personal
background sometimes damns a player who has the necessary
football qualifications.

BERNARD JOY, *Forward, Arsenal!*, **1952**.

Food may be incidental to some people, but to footballers who
have to keep in good physical trim it is extremely important. A
Continental breakfast is not very filling, but requests for a 'decent
breakfast' of ham and eggs met with uncomprehending stares.

BILLY LIDDELL, Liverpool and Scotland winger, on trip to Yugoslavia in 1955, in
My Soccer Story, **1960**.

My only problem seems to be with Italian breakfasts. No matter
how much money you've got, you can't seem to get any Rice
Crispies.

LUTHER BLISSETT, just after his transfer from Watford to Milan, **1983**.

The main thing I miss about London? The sausages.

TERRY VENABLES on life with Barcelona, **1984**.

Quite a few of them (footballers) can knock back a pint or two, but none are alcoholics.

JIMMY HILL, then Fulham player, in *Striking For Soccer*, **1961**.

While with Spurs I drank heavily to help relieve the pressure of big-time football. My career covered an era when the game suddenly went sick and defeat became a dirty word. We used to get really stoked up for the games, with our adrenalin pumped so high that a lot of us needed an after-match drink to bring us back to earth.

JIMMY GREAVES in *This One's on Me*, **1979**.

From what I have seen, the young players of today drink a lot more than during my teenage-to-early-twenties period. We used to be pint sinkers but now the orders are more likely to be Bacardi-and-cokes or gin-and-tonics. I have seen them pay out in a single round what I used to earn in a week at Chelsea.

JIMMY GREAVES in *This One's on Me*, **1979**.

If I go into a bar and have a lager shandy, word goes back that I'm knocking back bottles of champagne. By the time it gets to the papers or my manager at Arsenal, it's me lying in the gutter.

CHARLIE NICHOLAS, **1984**.

I don't drink every day, but when I do it's usually for four or five days on the trot. I've got a drink problem.

GEORGE BEST, **1979**.

I might go to Alcoholics Anonymous, but I think it'd be difficult for me to be anonymous.

BEST, **1980**.

Best wasn't the first player to be ruined by drink. I see booze as
one of the major evils of the game. And its influence has become
more widespread now there is big money to be earned. In my day
it was half a lager. Today they're drinking spirits.

BOBBY ROBSON in *Time on the Grass*, **1982**.

Some of the Altrincham players had big bellies and one of their
defenders looked nearer 40 than 30.

JIM HAGAN, Birmingham defender, on the Gola League team who knocked then-
First Division Birmingham out of the FA Cup, **1986**.

Professional athletes don't need healthy bodies, they do it all
with their minds. That is why experience is such an important
commodity. The body wears out quickly, but with training and
chemicals the mind is conditioned not to notice.

PETER GENT, ex-Dallas Cowboys player, in **1973** novel *North Dallas Forty*.

It was a different world in those days. Our big night out was fish
and chips and a pint, now it's the Top of the Town or whatever
it's called. They take taxis here, chauffeurs even, drink wine, and
as for the clothes, well it's a completely changed life today.

PAT WELTON, Spurs youth manager, **1972**.

My retirement plans are already being hampered by international
commitments. It's playing havoc with my golf schedule.

PAT JENNINGS on continuing to play for Northern Ireland after his official
retirement, **1985**.

The mesmeric effect of flickering flames can cure a bad patch by
helping players rehearse moves in their minds.

JOHN SYER, sports psychologist and adviser to Spurs, who advocates players
mentally rehearsing their moves, **1985**.

I think all our players have central heating.

PETER SHREEVE, Spurs manager.

From the first time I kicked a ball as a pro nineteen years ago, I began to learn what the game was all about. It's about the drunken parties that go on for days. The orgies, the birds and the fabulous money. Football is just a distraction – but you're so fit you can carry on with all the high living in secret, and still play the game at the highest level.

PETER STOREY, former Arsenal and England player, **1980**.

When Sam Jones and I arrived at Bloomfield Road in the morning for training, the rest of the lads used to chant: 'They don't drink. They don't smoke. They don't go out with women. What do they live for?' There was a one-word answer to that – football.

PETER DOHERTY, Blackpool, Northern Ireland and a self-confessed fitness freak, on football in the 1930s in *Blackpool Football* by Robin Daniels, **1972**.

I don't have any sort of drink problem, though if it helps to not touch a drop I'll try it. But if sex ruined your game, all the married players would be out of a job.

CHARLIE NICHOLAS, **1984**.

Of course a player can have sexual intercourse before a match and play a blinder. But if he did it for six months he'd be a decrepit old man. It takes the strength from the body.

BILL SHANKLY, **1971**.

One bloke admitted he didn't feel right unless he had a bit of sex on Saturday mornings. OK that's fine by me. . .if a player likes a ciggie or two, or a pint at lunchtime or a jump before breakfast that's his business.

TERRY JONES, Tividale manager, in Brian James, *Journey to Wembley*, **1977**.

I live only for football.

ROBERTO FALCAO, Roma and Brazil player, denying accusations of an extra-marital affair, **1983**.

If you think champagne, you drink champagne. At Sunderland they think water.

IAN ATKINS, Everton reserve defender, on his previous club, **1985**.

Some players' wives were in the best seats and others were near the corner flag. It was a right mess-up, typical of this club.

SUNDERLAND PLAYER on the Milk Cup final, **1985**.

We went into the dressing-room after training to find a notice informing us that because of economy cuts we were no longer to have a bath.

COLIN WEST, Sunderland forward, **1980s**.

I know of no class of work people who are less able to look after themselves than footballers; they are like a lot of sheep. A representative from the union could go and speak to them on why and wherefore they should join, and they would immediately decide to join. Two minutes after, a manager could go and say a few words to them, and they would decide not to join.

CHARLIE ROBERTS in *Football Players' Magazine*, **1914**.

I stand here as the representative of the last bonded men in Britain – the professional footballers! We seek your help to smash a system in which human beings are being bought and sold like cattle. A system which, as in feudal times, binds a man to one master or, if he rebels, stops him getting another job. The conditions of the footballer's employment are akin to slavery.

JIMMY GUTHRIE, Chairman of the Association Footballers' and Trainers' Union (forerunner of the Professional Footballers' Association), in speech to TUC at Southport, **1955**.

Many things are wrong with the British contract system, but the PFA are not militant enough and there is a complete lack of communication among the rank and file. . . . In any other business I could resign from the company and take a job elsewhere. . . . My generation will not put up with it.

DUNCAN McKENZIE, **1974**.

He is the Arthur Scargill of football.

ALAN MULLERY, Crystal Palace manager, on PFA secretary Gordon Taylor, **1983**.

Mr [Jimmy] Hill seems to wear so many different hats, it's untrue. I can remember when he was chairman of the Professional Foot- ballers' Association he fought for the abolition of the maximum wage for players. Spiralling wages have subsequently become one of the biggest problems in football, and now we find that Mr Hill is trying to get some restraint. Also, in 1978 when the PFA wanted to control transfer fees, he was against it. Shortly afterwards the transfer market went through the ceiling.

JOHN McGRATH, Port Vale manager, **1983**.

When I first played for my village side I was rewarded with a bag of vegetables and sixpence. At seventeen I was paid £5, and I counted it a dozen times on the way home, thinking I was in the big money. I suppose I was what they call a 'hungry fighter'.

JOE MERCER in *Soccer the British Way*, **1963**.

Times were hard for many people. Most of us were brought up to accept discipline, and to discipline ourselves. We didn't have much, so we learned to make the most of what we did have, and if a man was lucky enough to have a job he put everything into it. As a footballer, people looked up to you. No player was going to let that go.

GEORGE MALE, Arsenal and England full-back, on life in the **1930s**.

This fear of losing one's job manifested itself when the new contracts were being considered around 1 April each year. At that time of the season all the players, even the stars, were looking into the assistant secretary's office almost every day, asking if there was any news of their contracts. All of them carried an innate fear of not being offered fresh terms for the following season.

BOB WALL, Arsenal secretary, on Arsenal in the 1930s, in *Arsenal from the Heart*, **1969**.

The worst contract I have ever seen.

LORD WALTER MONCKTON, QC on the Football League forms, **1947**.

I used to take a part-time job away from soccer in summer. We had a supporter who owned a dairy, so a few of us would take jobs as drivers on his milk floats. Other lads would work in the pottery industry around Stoke and Burslem. We had to work or go without.

ROY SPROSON, Port Vale player **1949–71**, on life in the lower-divisions before the abolition of the maximum wage.

Some folks tell me that we professional players are soccer slaves. Well, if this is slavery, give me a life sentence.

BOBBY CHARLTON, **1960**.

I do not mind being a reserve. Even should I be kept as a reserve I will not return to Brazil. I prefer being here to playing in the best Brazilian team, for many reasons – but the main one is that I earn ten times as much as I could ever earn at home.

CANARIO, Real Madrid, **1961**.

Johnny Haynes is a top entertainer and will be paid as one from now on. I will give him £100 a week to play for Fulham.

TOMMY TRINDER, Fulham chairman, after lifting of the maximum wage in **1961**.

Italian players wonder how on earth players like Haynes live on such a salary! If anyone suggested that the Italians should play a whole season and bank only £5000, plus another £90 or so in bonuses, there would be a nationwide strike.

JOHN CHARLES, Juventus and Wales, in *The Gentle Giant*, **1962**.

Twenty pounds a week in the season, and £17 in summer, was no kind of money for men who gave pleasure to millions, and I was the last to blame them for wanting to change things. But the agreement the players won has allowed them to take more money out of the game than it has to give.

ALAN HARDAKER, Football League secretary, on the lifting of the maximum wage in 1961, in *Hardaker of the League*, **1977**.

Last year I picked up £1200 from Bells. And I've just had a tax bill for £992. I'll fight it. . .but you wonder what's the use of even going to lunch to pick up the prizes when that happens. There was no point my taking a rise [after succeeding Bill Shankly], the tax man would have grabbed it all back.

BOB PAISLEY in Brian James, *Journey to Wembley*, **1977**.

Players shouldn't need 'extras'. But then you don't see what the tax man does to their wage packets. It's bloody outrageous – they could earn a fortune this year with the treble, and they'll keep about a quarter of it. . . . That's why they turn up at a shop-opening for a hundred quid. Those fees come in readies.

PAISLEY on the players' 'pool' fifteen days before the 1976–77 FA Cup final, as above.

To fleece the public, that's why. They make so much out of a final they are greedy and want more.

BOB PAISLEY on the FA decision to stage an FA Cup final replay, if necessary, on 27 June **1977**, as above.

Anybody who complains about that sort of life wants his head examining.

TONY KAY, Sheffield Wednesday player, on the footballer's lot in **1962**. Three years later Kay received a life ban and prison sentence for his part in a bribes scandal.

If Mr Football Fan went to many a club car park when the players are rolling up for training he would probably be unable to restrain himself from a muttered 'Cor, Blimey'. For he'd see a fair number of the 'slaves' turning up for their daily stint in nice, shiny cars. At my own club, for instance, many of the lads have cars. I have myself, I'll admit. . . .

RONNIE CLAYTON, Blackburn Rovers and England player, in *A Slave – To Soccer*, **1960**.

The buying and selling of players sounds rather like a slave market. Moreover the payment of large transfer fees can be the refuge of the incompetent manager.

SIR NORMAN CHESTER, Chairman of committee examining English soccer's problems, **1968**.

For the next three years I am not a man, I am not a footballer, I am an industry.

JOHAN CRUYFF on signing for Barcelona, **1973**.

Take away Match of the Day and all the hangers-on and it's all very empty and lonely being a footballer.

RODNEY MARSH, **1971**.

The image of the professional footballer as a glamorous show-business type, surrounded by pretty girls and flash cars, is firmly implanted in most people's minds. I know him more accurately as the deeply insecure family man or the tearful, failed apprentice.

EAMON DUNPHY on the role of the PFA, **1973**.

It's like turtles in the South Sea. Thousands are hatched on the beaches, but few of them reach the water.

STEVE COPPELL, England international and PFA official, on career prospects for young players, **1983**.

At Burnley, no moustaches, no sideburns, long hair discouraged. . . . But when I was at Chelsea I could go through the menu, wine and all, 'phone home for hours, entertain friends, all on the club. If I run up a 2p phone call with Burnley, I get the bill. Keeps your feet on the ground, that, I'm telling you.

COLIN WALDRON, Burnley defender, 1975.

The permissive society has given us young footballers totally concerned with what they can get rather than what they ought to be giving.

BERTIE MEE, Arsenal manager, 1974.

To a certain extent football is still like white slavery. We are entertainers, playing to packed galleries every Saturday and often in between. People flock from all four corners of the country to see us perform, to see what it is that makes us stand out from the crowd. But our earnings are unrelated to our crowd-pulling power. . . . It makes me smile when people talk about big-money footballers.

BILLY BREMNER in the programme for his testimonial match in 1974, which earned him £40,000.

Of course I'm against Sunday soccer. It'll spoil my Saturday nights.

JOHN RITCHIE, Stoke centre-forward, 1974.

I cannot feed my child on glory.

PAOLO ROSSI during pay dispute with Juventus, 1982.

Two months ago Rossi was over the moon – now he is asking for it.

JUVENTUS official, replying to Italy's World Cup hero, 1982.

I personally don't hold with those players who say they'd play for England for nothing. So would I in one way. I'd play for Ireland for nothing, if they let everybody in for nothing. If they're collecting a £50,000 gate, playing for hope and glory has nothing to do with the facts.

DANNY BLANCHFLOWER in *The Encyclopedia of Association Football*, **1960**.

If patriotism is silly, then OK, we're silly. When we go onto the field for Scotland, we're ready to give blood. Of course, we'd like a lot of money, but even without it we'll play till we drop.

DAVID HAY, Scottish international, during **1974** World Cup finals in West Germany.

People say we do not have the passion to win a World Cup, that it does not mean enough to us. But to me it means everything, the absolute climax of a footballer's career. Club football gives us good rewards. I earn more than £1500 a week with PSV Eindhoven. But the final is above money. This is the end. On Sunday I will give everything.

WILLY VAN DER KERKHOF, Dutch midfield player, before the **1978** World Cup final against Argentina.

WANTED
Young man 15–20 years of age
Character – unimportant – can be manufactured
QUALIFICATIONS
Must have good lungs:
　　　　　　　　May be immersed in a bath of waste for
　　　　　　　　up to five years and come up smiling.
Must be flexible:
　　　　　　　　May have to bend over backwards.
Must be respectful of men:
　　　　　　　　with proven ability to stand the course.
Apply in whisky, brandy or any other suitable drink.
　　　　　　　　Soft drinks not accepted.

JOHN FARMER, former England Under-23 and Stoke goalkeeper, in his poem, 'To Answer Advertisements at 17 Years of Age!!'.

You drop your shoulder and move round a defender only to discover he didn't read your first dummy. So you crash straight into him and he comes out with the ball.

TREVOR BROOKING on playing Sunday-morning football for Havering Nalgo, **1985**.

I'm sure Sunday morning players get more pleasure than professionals.

JIMMY PEARCE, Spurs winger, in Hunter Davies, *The Glory Game*, **1972**.

I never say I'm going to *play* football. It's work.

MIKE ENGLAND, Spurs and Wales player, in Hunter Davies, *The Glory Game*, **1972**.

It's not money. The taxman takes half. . . . I sometimes wonder why I give myself two or three hours' driving on top of a day's work just to come here and train. When I get here, I know. It's not for the few quid. . .it's for the football. Knocking a ball about, having a laugh with your mates, getting out of the shower feeling shattered, but alive.

KEN MALLENDER, ex-Sheffield United defender, on playing non-League for Telford, in Brian James, *Journey to Wembley*, **1977**.

I don't like amateurs. They get up my nose. I know football as my living, as a hard life. . .my wife and child's livelihood. Football is a joy to them, plus a tenner in the boot as a bonus. And you can be the local hero in Hitchin or Wycombe. It's nice. No pressure. You have got your job and your family; so you can ponce around every Saturday, do a little bit, and you are a star. Amateurs' lives are a bit luxurious compared to ours.

EAMON DUNPHY in *Only a Game?*, **1976**.

If you think that Tividale doesn't matter because I've seen the big time you are wrong. At whatever level of football you are talking about everybody wants to play. I'd be as sick at missing the game at Oldbury as I used to be when I looked at the team sheet at St Andrews and saw eleven other names on the list.

DENNIS ISHERWOOD, ex-Birmingham full-back, on playing in the West Midland League for Tividale, in Brian James, *Journey to Wembley*, **1977**.

Funny thing is that, though it's not my living and the few quid I get is just an extra, I get as worked up as though the housekeeping money depended on every result. It's called being involved I suppose.

TERRY JONES, Tividale manager, in Brian James, *Journey to Wembley*, **1977**.

I shall never forget my second match for Brentford reserves.

JIMMY HILL in *Striking for Soccer*, **1961**.

The biggest difference betwen playing for Forfar and playing for Glasgow Rangers? Probably about two or three hundred pound a week.

STEWART KENNEDY, former Rangers and Scotland goalkeeper, **1984**.

A professional footballer has a duty to his wife and family to earn as much as he can from this sport as quickly as he can.

JOHN WARK on why his £50,000 salary at Ipswich was not enough, **1983**.

Have you noticed how we only win the World Cup under a Labour government?

RT HON HAROLD WILSON MP, Leader of the Opposition, **1971**.

Labour. Definitely. Aren't all the players Labour?

STEVE PERRYMAN, Spurs player, on his politics, in Hunter Davies, *The Glory Game*, **1972**. Two team-mates shared his views; nine were Tories.

I have never voted anything but Labour in my life. And I never will.

KEVIN KEEGAN, **1980**.

As they wheeled me out of hospital, everybody was looking at me quietly – 'poor chap' – and I didn't want it. I felt, psychologically, as though I needed to do something violent to myself.

STEVE COPPELL, on enforced retirement at the age of 27, **1983**.

The tragedy hasn't been forgotten, it never will be. But it's just a file of papers in somebody's in-tray now.

TREVOR CHERRY, Bradford City manager, reflecting in November on government promises after the fire which killed more than 50 fans in May, **1985**.

If this is what soccer is to become, let it die.

L'EQUIPE editorial after European Cup final disaster had claimed 39 lives, **1985**.

5
Philosophers All

Or Fred Malaprop played right-back for Port Vale

If ye dinnae score, ye dinnae win.

JIMMY SIRREL, Notts County manager, **1983**.

What do you have at Middlesbrough? Golden corner competitions?

KEVIN KEEGAN to former Liverpool colleague Phil Boersma during one of Middlesbrough's more negative displays under Jack Charlton, **1970s**.

> Often
> looking back
> along the wide expanse
> we conquered I see
> the dizzy heights we scaled,
> feel
> the pain of losing
> and hear the common bonds
> and sounds
> of a language never
> needing voices.
> No things to come
> can dull my feelings now
> or erase
> from my memory
> the better days.

JOHN FARMER, looking back on his career after Stoke's signing of Peter Shilton prompted him to retire, in his poem, 'In the Making of a Decision'.

When their second goal went in, I knew our pig was dead.

DANNY WILLIAMS, Swindon Town manager, after Swindon 1, West Ham United 2, FA Cup fourth-round replay **1974-75**.

His problem was that they kept passing the ball to his wrong feet.

LEN SHACKLETON on an unidentified player.

The penalty's the one thing keepers *don't* fear, because they can't lose. If it is scored, no-one blames him. If he saves it, he's a hero.

DAVE SEXTON, QPR manager, on Wim Wenders' film, *Goalkeeper's Fear of the Penalty*, **1975**.

A penalty is a cowardly way to score.

PELE, **1966**. His thousandth goal came from the spot.

The missing of chances is one of the mysteries of life.

SIR ALF RAMSEY, **1972**.

Being given chances and not taking them – that's what life is all about.

RON GREENWOOD, England manager, **1982**.

We looked bright all week in training, but the problem with football is that Saturday always comes along.

KEITH BURKINSHAW, Spurs manager, **1983**.

Football's not a matter of life and death. It's much more important than that.

BILL SHANKLY.

I'll stay in football. I don't mind if they stand me up and use me as a corner flag.

DEREK DOOLEY, Sheffield Wednesday centre-forward, after having right leg amputated, **1983**.

All-out attack mixed with caution.

JIM McLAUGHLIN, Shamrock Rovers manager, on his tactics for European tie, **1985**.

Soccer is the biggest thing that's happened in creation, bigger than any 'ism' you can name.

ALAN BROWN, Sunderland manager, **1968**.

Fishing and nature, especially birds, I have loved, although the one passion of my life has been football – the most exhilarating game I know, and the strongest protest against selfishness, without sermonizing, that was ever put before a thoughtful people.

JOHN GOODALL, Preston, Derby and England player, 1889–98, in Andrew Ward and Anton Rippon, *The Derby County Story*, **1983**.

All that I know most surely about morality and the obligations of man, I owe to football.

ALBERT CAMUS, **1957**. Camus, French philosopher-novelist, kept goal for Oran FC in Algeria.

I go much faster
Than those who run
Without thinking

PELE, *My Life and the Beautiful Game*, **1977**.

No player, manager, director or fan who understands football, either through his intellect or his nerve-ends, ever repeats that piece of nonsense, 'After all, it's only a game.' It has not been only a game for eighty years: not since the working classes saw in it an escape route out of drudgery and claimed it as their own.

ARTHUR HOPCRAFT in *The Football Man*, **1968**.

Now that the brief visit of the Dynamo team has come to an end it is possible to say publicly what many people were saying privately before the Dynamos ever arrived. That is, that sport is an unfailing cause of ill-will, and that if such a visit as this had any effect at all on Anglo-Soviet relations, it could only be to make them worse than before.

GEORGE ORWELL in *Tribune*, **1945**.

Even if George Orwell's Big Brother is ruling us in 1984, people will still be talking about football.

NEIL FRANKLIN, Stoke and England centre-half, in *Soccer at Home and Abroad*, **1956**.

I just happen to be one of those people for whom sport is on the highest possible plane. In a way, I see sport as being something even above real life.

DAVE SEXTON, Manchester United manager, **1980**.

Q: You are a Catholic. Are you a good Catholic?
A: At the moment, not very good, but I intend to do something about that. One thing I do miss – the traditional Tridentine Mass.

TOMMY DOCHERTY, in an interview with the *Sunday Mail*, **1980**.

God's judgement, which according to classic myths is part of every battle between two peoples, willed that luck fell on the German side in the game.

CHANCELLOR HELMUT SCHMIDT in telegram to President Mitterrand after West Germany's penalties' win in World Cup semi-final *v*. France, **1982**.

I talk a lot. On any subject. Which is always football.

TOMMY DOCHERTY, **1967**.

Now we have got to climb K2 and Everest in a week, but we can do it.

JOE MERCER on Manchester City's last two matches leading up to their League championship in **1968**.

Each season is like a woman having a baby. Winning the Cup was a nice baby. At the moment our baby is the stand. It is a bit of a jumbo and there is a hell of a problem with delivery.

DAVE SEXTON, Chelsea manager, on the club's multi-million-pound West Stand, **1973**.

Outside of family life, there is nothing better than winning European Cups.

BRIAN CLOUGH, **1980**.

There are no action replays in Heaven so you might as well enjoy playing and managing while you can. Football has let me live in style, but I should still have savoured it if the rewards had been a Mini rather than a Jaguar.

TERRY NEILL, **1974**.

Football is life. Life is not football. I often think on this. I wrestle with its problem. My deepest inner soul must know the answers. Do away goals count double in the Texaco Cup? How many points do I get if I'm booked for dissidence? Ah! Bollocks ter dis, I'm goin' ter de ale 'ouse fer a few bevvies!

SCOUSE BENNY in 'Gogols Are My Business', *Foul!* magazine, **1974**.

I suppose I'll have to get used to being addressed as 'Sir', but if a player gets formal on the field I will clobber him.

SIR ALF RAMSEY on being knighted in **1967**. Max Marquis, *Anatomy of a Football Manager*, **1970**.

Amateurism and good sportsmanship. . .for this club one is value-less without the other and, if either is surrendered, even in the present difficult world, in the cause of success, the time has surely been reached for the club's life, at least at senior level, to be brought to a close. Euthanasia must come before corruption.

CORINTHIAN-CASUALS centenary brochure, **1983**.

Football is a much more cynical game all round.

PHIL NEALE, Lincoln defender and Worcestershire cricketer, **1982**.

There is more to life than cricket.

IAN BOTHAM on turning out for Scunthorpe reserves, **1980**.

When a team is successful it's like rowing a boat. When you get the speed up, you begin to rest on the oars. And eventually the boat begins to slow down.

DANNY BLANCHFLOWER in *The Encyclopedia of Association Football*, **1960**.

And they were lucky to get nil.

LEN SHACKLETON after his six-goal debut for Newcastle in 13–0 defeat of Newport, **1946**.

I wouldn't check on a player I'm interested in under floodlights. He would look better than he really is.

BILLY WALKER, Nottingham Forest manager, **1960**.

He thought he was playing 4–2–4 in a five-a-side match.

SPEAKER at Liverpool Ramblers FC dinner, **1967**.

We were undone by the mass psychology of losing. If you're winning you get a snowball of the right attitudes. The average player becomes a good player and the good player becomes excellent. When you fail, it's the same principle in reverse.

IAN GREAVES, the manager who took Huddersfield and Bolton up to the First Division in the **1970s** – and back down.

Wait till we play them at The Valley.

CHRIS CATTLIN, Brighton manager, on a 5–3 home defeat in **1985** by Charlton . . . who had left The Valley two weeks earlier.

You don't hear people singing You'll Never Walk Alone at
Charlton home games too often.

LENNIE LAWRENCE, Charlton manager, soon after the club's move to Selhurst
Park, **1985**.

I put the ball past the goalkeeper. It's my one regret in all this
that the ball didn't finish in the net.

DEREK DOOLEY on the incident which led to his leg being amputated, in Arthur
Hopcraft, *The Football Man*, **1968**.

What wonderful goals. You really ought to take a closer look at
them.

SIR NEVILLE HENDERSON, British Ambassador in Berlin, offering his binoculars to
Goering during England's 6–3 win *v*. Germany, **1938**.

Our interpreter was on his usual hobby-horse, telling a few of the
lads of the tremendous good Russia was doing in the world today,
when in typical down-to-earth Lancashire fashion, my room-mate
Tommy Banks (Bolton Wanderers) interrupted with, 'Ay, that's
all very well, but what about Hungary!'

TOM FINNEY, in *Finney on Football*, **1958**.

I thought the No. 10, Whymark, played exceptionally well.

RT HON. MRS MARGARET THATCHER MP, at the FA Cup final, **1978**. Whymark, listed
in the programme, didn't play.

I hope Mrs Thatcher was watching.

GARY LINEKER after his hat-trick for England *v*. Turkey. His £800,000 transfer
from Leicester to Everton had been used as a stick to beat football with by
the Government, **1985**.

The politicians, the police and Uncle Tom Cobley and all lay the blame for hooliganism squarely on football clubs. Even their own governing body appeared to wilt under the pressure when it fined impecunious Millwall £7,500 for an attack on the police by hooligans at Luton, some 40 miles from their ground. Where is the justice in this? How can Millwall possibly be held responsible? The yobs, of course, got off scot-free and lived to fight another day.

GEORGE CUBITT, deputy chairman of the Central Council of Physical Recreation, **1985**.

We are opposed to FIFA's over-reaction. One even wonders whether it is political.

PETER ROBINSON, Liverpool chief executive, on the worldwide ban on English clubs in the wake of the Brussels disaster.

I hope she (Mrs Thatcher) is not going to be two-faced enough to turn up in the Royal box at the next FA Cup Final, because she hasn't been football's friend.

BRIAN CLOUGH on the government response to the Bradford and Brussels disasters.

I know more about football than politics.

RT HON. HAROLD WILSON MP, **1974**.

The politics involved make me nostalgic for the Middle East.

DR HENRY KISSINGER after FIFA rejected his USA bid to stage **1986** World Cup.

There's a hell of a lot of politics in football. I don't think Henry Kissinger would have lasted forty-eight hours at Old Trafford.

TOMMY DOCHERTY, **1982**.

I will never return to play in England – even if they gave me all the money in the world.

OSVALDO ARDILES as reported in an Argentinian newspaper, June **1982**.

I can't wait to get back. Every night I go to bed dreaming of Wembley.

ARDILES in December **1982**.

The trouble that day was that they used an orange-coloured ball. Eric Caldow and I (the full-backs) were afraid to kick it and Billy McNeill (of Celtic) was afraid to touch it.

BOBBY SHEARER, Glasgow Rangers defender, on Scotland's 9–3 defeat by England at Wembley, **1961**.

To be defeated by the United States at football was like the MCC being beaten by Germany at cricket.

BILLY WRIGHT on the USA's 1–0 win over England in 1950 World Cup, in *Captain of England*, **1950**.

Four of those goals came from outside our penalty area. We should never have lost.

SIR ALF RAMSEY, reflecting in **1966** on Hungary's 6–3 win over England at Wembley, **1953**.

We did not win anything. But as the Cinderella of the soccer world, we made quite a stir at the ball.

DANNY BLANCHFLOWER on Northern Ireland's success in reaching the World Cup quarter-final in Sweden, **1958**.

It is our new tactics. We equalize before the others have scored.

BLANCHFLOWER, **1958**.

I feel like jumping over the moon.

ALF RAMSEY, after Ipswich's League championship success in **1962** – an early case of soccer moon-leaping.

I am not one to jump over the moon or off a cliff.

SIR ALF RAMSEY, **1973**.

The Empire is gone. The pound is going down – and now even skirts seem to be. The Beatles were hooted out of Manila and the national cricket team is currently getting clobbered by the West Indies. Still, England oscillates. The cause of the excitement is an ugly, twelve-inch high trophy known as the World Cup and symbolic of supremacy in soccer – a game that seems tame to Americans but is still the most popular spectator sport on earth. In London, after years of trying, England finally won the World Cup.

Time magazine, **1966**.

England's victory could be a decisive factor in strengthening sterling. . .It was a tremendous, gallant fight that England won. Our men showed real guts and the bankers, I suspect, will be influenced by this, and the position of the Government correspondingly strengthened.

RICHARD CROSSMAN MP, Labour minister, in *Diaries of a Cabinet Minister, 1964–70.*

And does it mean anything except that we've got a good football team and an even better manager in Alf Ramsey? Probably not, although I'd like to draw the moral (not for the first time) that there's nothing wrong with Britain; it's just our politicians that let us down.

NIGEL LAWSON, later a Conservative minister, in *The Spectator*, **1966**.

As we came round the corner from the eighteenth green a crowd of members were at the clubhouse window cheering and waiting to tell me that England had won the World Cup. It was the blackest day of my life.

DENIS LAW, Scottish international and patriot, in *An Autobiography*, **1979**.

You've beaten them once. Now go out and bloody beat them again.

ALF RAMSEY to England team before extra time in **1966** World Cup final.

You must be f – joking.

SIR ALF RAMSEY, after being told 'Welcome to Scotland' at Prestwick Airport by a Scots journalist, **1967**.

It will be difficult for us to retain the World Cup, but it will be even more difficult to take it away from us.

SIR ALF RAMSEY, **1969**.

We are the best footballing nation in the world.

SIR ALF RAMSEY, two months after England failed to qualify for the World Cup in **1973**.

The real trouble with our national team is that in Italy we have fifty million advisers.

GIANNI RIVERA, Milan and Italy, **1969**.

It is a football match, not a war. Let's keep our sense of perspective – if we do lose, the game is not going to die. It will be a terrible thing for six weeks and then everyone will forget about it.

ALAN HARDAKER, Football League secretary, before England v. Poland, World Cup qualifier, **1973**.

It's worse than losing a war, a national crisis of the highest magnitude.

LORD WIGG after Poland had knocked out England, **1973**.

With a bit of luck in the World Cup I might have been knighted. Instead it looks as if I may be beheaded.

ALLY MacLEOD, Scotland manager, **1978**.

I'm finished with England. I'll never kick a ball for my country again. After ten years and sixty caps, I deserve better than to have to learn of my omission indirectly through the media.

KEVIN KEEGAN after being left out of Bobby Robson's first England squad, **1982**.

When you've been thrown out of clubs like Barrow and Southport, you learn to live with disappointment.

PETER WITHE, Aston Villa striker, on his omission from the same squad, **1982**.

If I win this one [getting the USA to the 1986 World Cup finals] they should send me to the Lebanon. I could run the whole damn country.

HOWARD SAMUELS, NASL president, **1983**.

It's like the difference berween a soldier walking through Alder-shot and one walking through Belfast. There's a state of mind necessary for the latter if you're to survive.

HOWARD WILKINSON, Sheffield Wednesday manager, on difference between First and Second Divisions, **1984**.

The theory that the League and Cup double will never be done in modern times is nonsense. I realize no one has done it for sixty years, but there is a simple explanation for that. No club has been good enough.

MATT BUSBY, after Manchester United had lost the **1957** FA Cup final and the chance of the double.

I believe the way things are now, the majority of clubs in the First Division could pull off the double.

DAVE SEXTON, Manchester United manager, **1979**.

For the little clubs the second round of the FA Cup is like swimming from a shipwreck only to find that the beach is mined.

ALEC STOCK, whose managerial career included epic Cup runs with Yeovil and Fulham.

Everybody knows you have to get out of the Third Division – it may not be here much longer.

JIM SMITH, Oxford United manager, **1982**.

League football is a rat-race of the first magnitude.

BOB LORD, Burnley chairman, **1968**.

It's a rat-race – and the rats are winning.

TOMMY DOCHERTY, **1982**.

I don't mind *what* you call me, so long as you don't call me late for lunch.

WILLIAM (FATTY) FOULKE, twenty-two-stone goalkeeper, **1901**.

When the ball is coming my way, I shut the other eye and play from memory.

BOB THOMSON, Chelsea's one-eyed centre-forward of **1915**.

Tha doesn't need to worry. I'll plonk two in in next half.

FRED TILSON of Manchester City to his goalkeeper Frank Swift at half-time in the **1934** FA Cup final. He did so.

PRINCESS MARGARET: But Mr Labone, where *is* Everton?
BRIAN LABONE: In Liverpool, Ma'am.
PRINCESS MARGARET: Of course, we had your first team here last year.

BILL SHANKLY story of **1966** FA Cup final.

I'm a people's man, a player's man. You could call me a humanist.

BILL SHANKLY, **1970**.

I suppose it will be an all-ticket match.

DANNY BLANCHFLOWER, on being put into the reserves.

Most Dangerous Opponent: My ex-wife.

FRANK WORTHINGTON, in answer to magazine questionnaire.

This team will dominate the seventies. . .nothing will stop it becoming one of the greatest club teams of all times.

MERSEYSIDE SOCCER CORRESPONDENT in **1970** on. . .Everton.

How could I avoid being Player of the Year playing behind our defence?

PAT JENNINGS, then of Spurs, accepting Footballer of the Year award, **1973**.

Stan Cummins will be Britain's first million-pound footballer.

JACK CHARLTON, Middlesbrough manager, **1978**.

People keep on about Total Football, but all I know about is Total Petrol.

DEREK DOUGAN, Wolves and Northern Ireland striker, **1973**.

People keep on about stars and flair. As far as I'm concerned you find stars in the sky and flair [sic] is something on the bottom of trousers.

GORDON LEE, Everton and Newcastle manager, **1970s**.

I've given him carte blanche, as Ron Greenwood used to say, though I didn't use that phrase in the dressing-room. Told him to go where he likes.

GEOFF HURST as manager of Telford, in Brian James, *Journey to Wembley*, **1977**.

That Johnny Giles of Leeds is a great player. Beats me why Alf Ramsey has never picked him for England.

WILLIE ORMOND, Scotland manager, **1973**.

I read in the newspapers that Terry Neill says he'll put the joy back in Tottenham's football. What's he going to do – give them bloody banjos?

EDDIE BAILY, ex-assistant manager of Spurs, **1974**.

That's typical of this club. For an extra £10,000 they could have got John Snow.

JEFF ASTLE, West Bromwich Albion striker, on hearing that Albion had signed Tranmere goalkeeper Jim Cumbes, a fast bowler with Lancashire, **1969**.

I've heard of players selling dummies, but this club keeps buying them.

LEN SHACKLETON, on Newcastle United.

Even when you're dead, you shouldn't let yourself lie down and be buried.

GORDON LEE, **1981**.

It's ridiculous, I've served more time than Ronnie Biggs did for the Great Train Robbery.

MALCOLM ALLISON, then Plymouth manager, appealing against his touchline ban, **1978**.

I have other irons in the fire, but I'm keeping them close to my chest.

JOHN BOND, on leaving Manchester City manager's job, **1983**.

I hope you both lose.

BILL SHANKLY to Joe Mercer before Derby County v. Manchester City, April **1972**, when Liverpool, Derby and City were chasing the championship.

Drop four players? I hate to make changes at all, and when they are necessary I try to arrange they cause as little disturbance as possible. If I were to make four alterations I would regard it as a confession that I had been seriously at fault before in judging the merits of the men.

HERBERT CHAPMAN, Arsenal manager **1930s**, on a supporter's suggestion for changes.

I don't drop players, I make changes.

BILL SHANKLY, **1973**.

REPORTER: It was a funny game, Jim.
JIMMY SIRREL: Human beings are funny people.

EXCHANGE after Arsenal *v.* Notts County match, **1982**.

Africa? We're not in bloody Africa, are we?

GORDON LEE, Everton manager, asked his impressions of Africa during tour of Morocco, **1978**.

Preston? They're one of my old clubs. But then most of them are. I've had more clubs than Jack Nicklaus.

TOMMY DOCHERTY, **1979**.

I've been in more courts than Bjorn Borg.

TOMMY DOCHERTY, **1981**.

Claim to fame outside soccer: I once put together an MFI wardrobe in less than four days.

TERRY GIBSON, Coventry striker, **1985**.

My ambition is to meet Prince Charles. I call him 'King'.

ALAN BALL, **1979**.

Never in the history of the FAI Cup had a team wearing hooped jerseys lost a final in a year ending in 5.

HOME FARM FC (Dublin) programme notes, **1985**.

Terrific. Now Liverpool can't do the double.

FRANK MCLINTOCK, Arsenal's double-winning captain in 1971, to the Arsenal players after they had beaten Liverpool in the **1980** FA Cup semi-final.

You'll never believe this Mum, but we've just beaten Liverpool.

JEFF WOOD, HJK Helsinki and ex-Charlton goalkeeper, phoning home after Liverpool's 1–0 European Cup defeat in Finland, **1982**.

My team won't freeze in the white-hot atmosphere of Anfield.

RON SAUNDERS, Aston Villa manager, **1980**.

We're halfway round the Grand National course with many hurdles to clear. So let's make sure we all keep our feet firmly on the ground.

MIKE BAILEY, Charlton manager, on his team's promotion chances, **1981**.

We're like Lady Di. She's not the Queen yet. She's not even married. But like us, she's nicely placed.

JIMMY SIRREL, Notts County manager, on his side's promotion prospects, **1981**.

Looking back, some of the pictures I've posed for have been daft.

CHARLIE NICHOLAS on eve of Arsenal debut, **1983**.

Canon League? Some teams are so negative they could be sponsored by Kodak.

TOMMY DOCHERTY on his return from Australia, **1983**.

Thank God for the Army. Otherwise I'd probably still be in Wales slogging it out in the mud and drinking ale. The Italian Army has a special regiment for soccer players, so all I did was train all day.

GIORGIO CHINAGLIA, ex-Swansea Town player, later of Lazio and New York Cosmos, **1979**.

When one door opens, another closes.

ALAN MULLERY after his Charlton team had beaten Barnsley at expense of five injuries, **1981**.

When one door opens, another smashes you in the face.

TOMMY DOCHERTY on his dismissal by Preston, **1981**.

In terms of a fifteen-round boxing match we're not getting past
the first round. The tempo is quicker. Teams will pinch your
dinner from under your noses. They don't give you a chance to
play. If you don't heed the warnings, you get nailed to the cross.

GORDON MILNE, Leicester manager, on his team's adjustment to the First Division
and after heavy home defeat, **1983**.

All the lads have been moaning about him. He dives in yards
from the ball and hits you on the legs whether the ball's there or
not. No one appreciates that kind of thing, especially in training.

ANONYMOUS BRIGHTON PLAYER on Hans Kraay Jr, Dutch player suspended in
Holland but on trial with Brighton, **1983**.

There is a rat in the camp trying to throw a spanner in the works.

CHRIS CATTLIN, Brighton manager, **1983**.

Football is the opera of the people.

STAFFORD HEGINBOTHAM, Bradford City chairman, **1985**.

It's a cross I'll have to bear. Unlike when I was playing – I couldn't
bear crosses then.

DAI DAVIES, ex-Everton and Wales goalkeeper, on having to take time off from
his bookshop to play for Bangor in Europe, **1985**.

We're expecting a lot of heavy praying.

ARCHIE PHILLIPS, Hereford director, after borrowing church pews for home FA
Cup tie with Arsenal, **1985**. Arsenal won 7–2 in replay.

What it all means is that from time to time you have to adjust
your expectation levels. And while expectation levels have always
to be high from the point of view of ambition targets, the achieve-
ment factor relative to expectations can only be along the lines of
your resources.

COLIN MURPHY, Lincoln manager, **1983**.

Obviously for Scunthorpe it would be a nice scalp to put Wimbledon on their bottoms.

DAVE BASSETT, Wimbledon manager, **1984**.

All visiting teams complain about the pitch – but they all seem to win.

ARCHBISHOP MAKARIOS to Dunfermline players visiting Cyprus for a European tie, **1968**. The Scots won 2–0. In Paterson and Scott, *Black and White Magic*.

If you have a fortnight's holiday in Dublin you qualify for an Eire cap.

MIKE ENGLAND who picked Belgian-born Pat van den Hauwe for Wales, **1986**.

Cricket shouldn't be used as a political football.

DAVID GRAVENEY, Gloucestershire captain, **1986**.

It only takes a second to score a goal.

BRIAN CLOUGH, **1984**.

The best team always wins. The rest is only gossip.

JIMMY SIRREL, Notts County manager, **1985**.

6
View from (and of) the Bridge

Next to being a City Alderman, one of the most pleasurable things of this life must be to have a seat on the board of the English Football Association or to be a leading member of some other leading Association body. There is no doubt that these big-wigs take full advantage of the various outings, feeds etc etc, perhaps, after all, it is but natural.

Athletic Journal, **1890**.

This page has been left blank in accordance with the author's wishes.

PUBLISHER'S FOOTNOTE to chapter heading, 'The Average Director's Knowledge of Football', in Len Shackleton's *Clown Prince of Soccer*, **1955**.

When I came to Manchester as a 15-year-old from the North East, I didn't know what a director was or what he did. My dad would have explained it as someone who didn't work.

BOBBY CHARLTON on becoming a Manchester United director, **1985**.

I appeal to the authorities to release the brake which they seem to delight in jamming on new ideas. . .as if wisdom is only to be found in the council chamber.

HERBERT CHAPMAN, Arsenal manager, **1933**.

I am impatient and intolerant of much that seems to me to be merely negative, if not actually destructive, legislation.

HERBERT CHAPMAN, **1933**.

I have been with him when an old newspaper seller has turned to a pal, and, pointing to Wall, shouted, 'That's 'im! 'E's the kindest bloke in the world. It's 'im we've got to thank for keepin' ole Tom out o' the workhouse!'

F. B. DOUGLAS-HAMILTON on 'Sir Frederick Wall, the Soccer King' in *The Boy's Own Annual*, **1933–34**. Wall was FA secretary.

A man who gives himself up to football, body and soul. . .will take risks and get himself entangled in such a way as he would never dream of in the conduct of his own business.

SIR FREDERICK WALL, in *Fifty Years of Football*, **1935**.

Let club directors make a hash of the affairs of their own teams, but spare England the catastrophe of their attentions.

LEN SHACKLETON, **1958**.

From information I have picked up on my travels, I would say that England, Ireland (North and South), Wales and Scotland are the only countries in which the international team is chosen by men lacking an obvious footballing background. Surely that cannot be a good thing?

TOM FINNEY on the committees, composed of club directors, that picked the home nations' teams until the late **1950s**.

After a midweek game. . .Derby manager Harry Storer was driven to taking up the issue of England selection. He asked Joseph Richards (Barnsley chairman and Football League president) what right he had to be an England selector. When Richards told him he had been watching football for over fifty years. Storer was ready. 'Come off it,' he said. 'We've got a corner-flag at the Baseball Ground. It's been there for fifty years and still knows absolutely nothing about the game.'

ANDREW WARD and IAN ALISTER in *Barnsley – A Study in Football 1953–59*. The incident took place in **1957** after England's 3–2 home defeat by Northern Ireland.

When I made my debut [in 1959], the England side was picked
by a team of selectors. Most of them were elderly gentlemen, old
enough to be the grandfathers of the players they were selecting.
On one tour I recall one of the old boys praising the performance
of Ron Flowers after a match that Ron had watched from the
touchline bench.

JIMMY GREAVES in *This One's on Me*, **1979**.

Football is essentially a professional game but professional people
are not allowed to run it. All the ideas are the prerogative of the
butchers, bakers and candlestick-makers; help is never sought
from the players. Even when international teams are due to be
selected, club managers, players and ex-players (in other words
the only people qualified to be good judges of ability) must never
'interfere'.

JIMMY McILROY, Burnley and Northern Ireland player, in *Right Inside Soccer*,
1960. McIlroy's chairman at Burnley, Bob Lord, was a butcher.

I have loved football. I still love it. If I didn't, I couldn't tolerate
the way people treat me in the game.

DANNY BLANCHFLOWER in *The Encyclopedia of Association Football*, **1960**.

On return from New York I felt that whilst I cannot agree with
any of the principles of the Communist system – I deplore them,
I hate them, I think they are rotten – I felt that Kruschev is not
entirely to blame for the world situation.

BOB LORD, Burnley chairman, on his club's participation in a tournament in the
USA in 1960, in *My Fight for Football*, **1963**.

No charter for the players will do anything unless you have the
right men to run the game.

DANNY BLANCHFLOWER on the campaign to improve players' status in **1950–60s**.

I kept 20,000 tickets under my bed and sold every single one myself. I used to go home with the money stuffed in every pocket. . . . Crewe had no safe. Now that was a strain. And we lost 13–2. I bought Crewe a safe with the profits.

PETER ROBINSON, Liverpool managing director, on his early days as secretary of Crewe. The game referred to was Spurs 13, Crewe Alexandra 2, in 1960. Brian James, *Journey to Wembley*, **1977**.

Footballers couldn't run a fish and chip shop.

BOB LORD, Burnley chairman.

I wouldn't hang a dog on the word of an ex-professional footballer.

ALAN HARDAKER, Football League secretary.

I remember Joe Richards (League president) saying at one meeting: 'For the good of the game I suggest. . . .' Jimmy Hill (PFA chairman) cut across him: 'We're not interested in the good of the game. We're only here to talk about our members.' It was at this time I started fishing for sharks, and my first success was a beauty of just over a hundred pounds which I caught off the Cornish coast at Looe. We hauled it in and my partner gave it a good clout. 'Hit it again,' I said. 'It looks like Jimmy Hill.'

ALAN HARDAKER on the 1961 dispute over the maximum wage in *Hardaker of the League*, **1977**.

I hold that players are the club's best assets. If that is so, they must be dealt with grandly. We are not looking for a bargain, but for the great player, and he deserves everything that his rank and artistry can get.

DON RAIMUNDO SAPORTA, vice-president of Real Madrid, **1961**.

People still expect more of Arsenal than they do of most other teams. If one of our players commits a foul the other team's supporters are appalled.

DENIS HILL-WOOD. Old Etonian and Arsenal chairman, in Arthur Hopcraft, *The Football Man*, **1968**.

Your mouth is obviously bigger than mine. I suggest you run your club in your way and leave us to run ours.

ARTHUR WAIT, Crystal Palace chairman, in letter to Bob Lord, Burnley chairman, who had criticized Palace's high bonuses, **1970**.

You have to be crackers to be a director of a football club. Who'd pour money into football when you can earn 10 or 20 per cent with it?

ARTHUR WAIT, **1971**.

Soccer is run by second-rate con-men. Petit-bourgeois, frustrated small businessmen. It's a tragedy because socially football is very important.

EAMON DUNPHY, **1973**.

Football chairmen are almost to a man butchers and sausage-meat manufacturers, pork-pie impresarios, industrial and property moguls.

DAVID TRIESMAN, sociologist-journalist, in *Seven Days*, **1973**.

The Villa chairman, Doug Ellis, said he was right behind me. I told him I'd sooner have him in front of me where I could see him.

TOMMY DOCHERTY, **1970**.

I've sacked him [Clough] on three occasions in the last two years, and told him to bugger off out of the club.

SAM LONGSON, Derby County chairman, **1973**.

Playing football and making profits on Sundays is wrong. We will not disturb the peace and quiet of the neighbourhood of Highbury on that day.

BOB WALL, Arsenal secretary, **1973**.

The players get upset at the large gaps on the terraces, and under the floodlights they won't notice them so much.

RODNEY STONE, Charlton general manager, on why they were switching to Friday-night football, **1973**.

We don't recognize *any* supporters' associations. I don't mind them existing – just won't have anything to do with them. I never go to Supporters' Dinners; it only costs a fiver or so to go, but then they think they own you. In particular, I never accept money from supporters' associations; they hand you a couple of cheques for a few thousand, and the next thing you know they're demanding a seat on the Board in return. . .My ambition, what we are aiming for, is for the club to function completely without any money coming through the turnstiles at all. That is the road to Utopia.

BOB LORD, Burnley chairman, **1973**.

Of course we're going to continue competing in Europe. How else can we get our duty-free cigarettes?

JOHN COBBOLD, Ipswich chairman, **1973**.

You will train the players Allison, and I will pick the team.

TOMMY THOMPSON, then chairman of Pegasus (later Sir Harold Thompson, chairman of the FA), offering Malcolm Allison the job of coach to the great **1950s** Oxbridge amateurs. Allison told Thompson, 'in effect, to stuff Pegasus'.

Sir Harold Thompson, chairman of the FA, treated me like an employee. These Arab Sheikhs treat me like one of them.

DON REVIE, **1979**.

Even I could manage this lot.

SAM LONGSON, Derby chairman, after Brian Clough's departure, **1973**.

If people did not have the filthy, dirty habit of smoking, there would be 56 people alive today.

STAFFORD HEGINBOTHAM, Bradford City chairman, after the fire disaster, **1985**.

I could understand why Brian [Clough] hardly ever went to board meetings at Derby, because while I was there I found it difficult to get any sense out of them. There was one director who used to snoop about the dressing-rooms and kitchens. He'd go into the kitchen and say to the woman in charge, 'I see you've got an extra bottle of brandy – where did you get that from?' It was like having a spy walking around.

TOMMY DOCHERTY in *Call The Doc*, **1981**.

One wonders today, however, what some businesses would be like if they were run on the same haphazard lines as most football clubs still are. The amateur director has been kicked out of most industrial and commercial boardrooms. But not in football.

DEREK DOUGAN in *Football as a Profession*, co-authored with Percy M. Young, **1974**.

While I was in the car park the directors all trooped out to join the coach and they walked past me without a single word of greeting. I never even got a good morning from one of them. It was as though I didn't exist. If somebody had stuck a knife in me at that moment, it couldn't have hurt me more.

PAT JENNINGS, Spurs goalkeeper, on learning that the club didn't want him any more, **1977**.

I was watching a game at Fulham and saw Alan Mullery punch one of his own players for not trying. I thought, 'Christ, this man is dedicated.'

MIKE BAMBER, Brighton chairman, on how he came to make Mullery manager in **1976**.

The ideal board of directors should be made up of three men – two dead and the other dying.

TOMMY DOCHERTY, **1977**.

When you engage a man you have full confidence in as manager, then you allow him to manage and abide by his decisions and judgement.

MANNY CUSSINS, Leeds United chairman, who had already sacked managers Clough and Armfield and later dismissed Clarke and Adamson, **1979**.

You could put his knowledge of the game on a postage stamp. He wanted us to sign Salford Van Hire because he thought he was a Dutch international.

FRED EYRE, former assistant manager at Wigan, on a powerful director, **1981**.

I wonder how the directors of Rochdale, Darlington and Crewe are encouraging their managers in what can be a very lonely job.

GEORGE KIRBY, Halifax Town manager, replying to criticism by the board in his programme notes, **1979**.

I've always dreamed of being able to take over a big club.

ANTON JOHNSON after buying Third Division Rotherham United for £62,000, **1979**.

Sacking the manager is not the answer to Fulham's or indeed football's problems. What went on at Manchester City and Palace recently is disgusting. So, for that matter, were the events at Norwich. Contracts should be honoured both ways.

ERNIE CLAY, Fulham chairman, two days before he dismissed manager Bobby Campbell, **1980**.

I don't feel under any pressure from the chairman. He has been great, like a father to me. People are saying I am living in the shadow of the sack. All I can say is that the chairman has told me I've got a contract with him for life.

BOBBY CAMPBELL shortly before he was sacked by Clay, **1980**.

Football hooligans? Well there are the ninety-two club chairmen for a start.

BRIAN CLOUGH, **1980**.

I have never been so insulted by anyone in football as this little upstart puppy.

DENIS HILL-WOOD, Arsenal chairman, announcing that he had written to FA asking them to charge Clough with bringing the game into disrepute, **1980**.

Brady's talent was just beyond my comprehension. The player I admired was Peter Storey. I used to play like that, I was fourteen stone stripped and I wanted the ball.

DENIS HILL-WOOD, **1981**.

The man who sacked me [at Fulham] was Eric Miller – you know, Sir Eric Miller, the property developer who shot himself. Shows how he reacted to pressure doesn't it?

BOBBY ROBSON, **1981**.

You've made bloody little difference.

SHEFFIELD UNITED DIRECTOR to Joe Mercer, after Mercer's first two games as manager had produced one point.

Well, the pressure is really on you now, son!

WIGAN ATHLETIC DIRECTOR to manager Larry Lloyd after the team's first defeat of the season, **1981**.

At other clubs the directors probably get worried if things aren't going well, and they don't like to have people coming up to them criticizing in pubs and at parties. Well, that doesn't influence me at all. If people start telling me what's wrong with the team I just say, 'Look, why don't you f – awff.'

PATRICK COBBOLD, Ipswich chairman, **1981**.

I might very well be able to talk a top manager like Brian Clough into coming to Boro, but what good would that do? I'd probably only get myself a bloke who wanted to keep me out of the way.

ALF DUFFIELD, Middlesbrough chairman, explaining his decision to appoint Willie Maddren as manager in **1985**. Eighteen months later Middlesbrough were relegated and Duffield resigned, having already sacked Maddren.

'In the last dozen years there has been a great change in the character of the paid player . . . We now see him able to take his position in the best of company.' William (Billy) Meredith, 1906

'An old newspaper seller shouted, "That's 'im! 'E's the kindest bloke in the world. It's 'im we've got to thank for keepin' ol' Tom out o' the workhouse!" ' F. B. Douglas-Hamilton on Sir Frederick Wall, the Soccer King of the early 1900s, pictured above

'I'm no angel, but I've never kicked anyone deliberately.' Billy Bremner in 1967. Here Bremner (*left*) plays guardian angel to Martin Chivers

'It's bloody tough being a legend.' Ron Atkinson, 1983. *Above.* the legend and companion

'I find it ironical that Brian Clough should call for a total ban on TV soccer after making the kind of money as a member of TV's World Cup panel that would seem a pools win to small clubs.' Derek Dougan, 1983. *Below,* Clough (*left*) and Dougan (*second left*) join the kipper tie brigade (*left to right*) Crerand, Moncur, Allison and Jack Charlton

'Tell the Kraut to get his ass up front. We don't pay a million for a guy to hang around in defense.' NY Cosmos executive on tendency of Franz Beckenbauer (*above*) to play deep

'The country which gave the world Disneyland has provided a Mickey Mouse football industry.' *Rothman's Football Yearbook 1979-80*

'Moscow think Marcus Allen (*above*) is a new secret weapon. They insist we dismantle it.' President Reagan, 1984

'The Man's Game For All The Family' Widnes *v.* Wigan, Wembley, 1984

'I was ugly enough through Rugby Union. I'd hate to think what I'd look like if I had ten years with the League.' Tommy David, who played professionally for Cardiff City, pictured during his Union days

'I wouldn't want to play rugby. That's a very dangerous game.' St Louis Cardinals player, 1983. *Above,* JPR Williams five years earlier, a victim of the 'hooligan's game played by gentlemen'

'Eddie Waring has done for Rugby League what Cyril Smith has done for hang-gliding.' Reggie Bowden, 1980. *Below,* the Fulham scrum-half achieves lift-off with help from the Hull pack

United have begun to think that 'class' is something which comes with big office suites and flash motor cars. . . . That great club is slowly being destroyed. And I blame one family for the ruin. The Edwards family. The master butchers of Manchester.

HARRY GREGG, former Manchester United goalkeeper, after his sacking by the club, **1981**.

We now have a rat-race with the top players demanding and getting £1000 a week.

PETER SWALES, Manchester City chairman, **1982**.

I told him not to be such a great big baby.

STAN SEYMOUR, Newcastle chairman, on Jack Charlton's resignation as manager, **1985**.

Peter Swales? He works hard. Likes publicity, though. He wears a card round his neck saying, 'In case of heart attack call a press conference.'

TOMMY DOCHERTY on the Manchester City chairman, **1982**.

If you thought Bob Lord was rude, you've heard nothing yet.

JOHN JACKSON, Burnley chairman, after row over tickets at Chelsea, **1982**.

When I was a director of Sheffield United for six months, the chairman told me normal business standards didn't apply in football. It was the most stupid advice I ever had.

MIKE WATTERSON, Derby chairman, **1982**.

The next time we need major surgery, could we have it on the National Health?

MANCHESTER UNITED SHAREHOLDER, after manager Ron Atkinson had explained the club's £2 million loss by saying the team had required 'major surgery' when he took over, **1982**.

I remember the late Alan Ball senior telling me what his chairman said to him when he was appointed manager of Preston. Posing for a photographer, the chairman put his arm round Alan and said, 'We sink or swim together.' Two years later, Alan was called in to see the board and knew in advance that they were going to sack him. He asked, 'How many of you are going to sink with me?' Of course none of them did.

BOBBY ROBSON, in *Time on the Grass*, **1982**.

The chairman [Mark Huyler] has assured me that my job is safe.

KEN CRAGGS, Charlton manager, the day before he was fired, **1982**.

The Super League idea has about as much chance of getting through as there is of Arthur Scargill admitting he needs a wig.

ERNIE CLAY, Fulham chairman, **1982**.

What chance have you got when the League president is chairman of Notts County? They average 8000 a match. He wants more football from his club, not less. Second-rate clubs will keep soccer in a second-rate situation.

KEITH BURKINSHAW, Spurs manager, **1982**.

We at Derby can say that we have not felt the pinch as much as other clubs and we have come to be recognized throughout this country and in Europe for what is good in football.

SAM LONGSON, Derby chairman, in the club's annual report, **1975**.

The company is in a precarious financial position. Additional funds are urgently required by the company in order substantially to reduce bank borrowings and interest charges to an acceptable level and to provide a more sound financial base for the company.

PROSPECTUS for the proposed issue of 60,000 shares in Derby, **1982**.

More and more clubs are being 'rescued' by rich men who take over as chairmen and expect the manager to chase honours. These people know little about the running of professional football and I see their entry into the game as a disquieting feature. I worked for one once, Sir Eric Miller at Fulham, and I will never work for one again. They appoint what I call box-office managers, front-of-house people who talk well in public, and they expect instant success. I prefer the Ipswich way, which is gradual evolution backed by financial prudence. We spend our money wisely, adding new stands, new facilities and developing young players.

BOBBY ROBSON, in *Time on the Grass*, **1982**.

You ask what constitutes a crisis here. Well, if we ran out of white wine in the boardroom.

PATRICK COBBOLD, Ipswich chairman, **1982**.

What we need now is money from the business community. Trouble is, the town has changed. The mills tend to be run from London, and I'm not sure the new owners care.

JOHN CROWTHER, Halifax Town vice-chairman, **1982**.

This is your club now. I love you all. I am going to come amongst you this afternoon.

DEREK DOUGAN chief executive, addressing Wolves crowd before first game after escape from liquidation, **1982**.

They have brought this town into disrepute, making Wolverhampton the butt of every comedian's joke. We must have a talk as soon as possible to find out where Allied Properties' interests lie. On Saturday's performance it is not in football.

JOHN BIRD, Wolverhampton Council leader, after Wolves' 5–0 defeat by Watford, **1983**.

It was a unanimous choice – which is unusual for us.

PETER SWALES, Manchester City chairman, on his board's appointment of John Benson as manager, **1983**.

I am struck by the parallels between the disorder which characterizes the approach of some football boardrooms and the disorderly behaviour of the minority of the game's followers.

NEIL MACFARLANE MP, Minister for Sport, **1983**.

If a chairman is to be held responsible for playing success or failure or indeed monotonous competence, I am prepared to stand up and be counted.

JIMMY HILL, after resigning as Coventry City chairman, **1983**.

It wasn't so much the death threats or the vandalism, but when you sit with your family in the directors' box and hear a couple of thousand people chanting 'Gilbert Blades is a wanker', then you feel it's time to go.

GILBERT BLADES, ex-Lincoln City chairman, on his resignation, in Anton Rippon, *Soccer: the Road to Crisis*, **1983**.

If we go all the way to Wembley, it's difficult to imagine the club looking elsewhere for a new manager.

MIKE BAMBER, Brighton chairman on Jimmy Melia's employment prospects at Brighton, March **1983**.

We might have got to Wembley, but you've got to remember we've only won seven out of thirty-six League games under Jimmy.

BRIGHTON DIRECTOR, on why Melia was sacked in October **1983**.

My chairman Robert Maxwell, they ought to let him run football.

JIM SMITH, Oxford United manager, **1983**.

I understand and sympathize with their strong feelings, but I cannot accept their conservatism or parochialism.

ROBERT MAXWELL on reaction of Oxford and Reading fans to proposed merger as Thames Valley Royals, **1983**.

Maxwell has the posture and manners of the dominant male.

DR DESMOND MORRIS, author of *The Naked Ape* and a co-director of Maxwell's at Oxford, **1983**.

I have played football since I was a toddler. Left wing, as you would expect. I was very fast.

ROBERT MAXWELL, **1985**.

He stole the glory from the players and spoiled a night that should have been for the players and supporters.

JIM SMITH, Oxford manager, on how Maxwell attacked the local council at the club's promotion celebrations, **1985**.

Only women and horses work for nothing.

DOUG ELLIS, Aston Villa's first paid director, **1983**.

The only way they [Nottingham Forest players] will get European bonuses is if the club's directors have a whip-round. But I've never seen pigs fly.

BRIAN CLOUGH, **1983**.

I missed the last goal. I was too busy counting our share of the money.

KEN BATES, Chelsea chairman, after Full Members final had produced receipts of £508,000, **1986**.

If twelve-year-olds could drive, we wouldn't have any problems getting crowds.

LEE STERN, Chicago Sting owner, on the growth of participation in youth soccer while NASL gates fell, **1983**.

We've got a long-term plan for this club and apart from the results it's going well.

ERNIE CLAY, Fulham chairman, **1980**.

I've heard claims that I'm supposed to be using Mafia money. Some football clubs are in such a mess right now you could buy them out of Brownie funds.

ANTON JOHNSON, then Rotherham chairman, on his part in club takeovers, **1983**.

We have no desire just to be a football club. That is not the basis of success.

PAUL BOBROFF, chairman of Tottenham Hotspur plc, **1983**.

My apologies to all of you for supporting us through this trying season.

VINCE BARKER, Hartlepool United chairman, in final programme of **1983–84**.

Most people who can remember when County were a great club are dead.

JACK DUNNETT, Notts County chairman, **1983**.

Football directors are nobody's friends except when there are Cup Final tickets to give away.

ROY HATTERSLEY MP in *Goodbye to Yorkshire*, **1976**.

7

He Who Must Be Obeyed

A considerable grievance to some gentlemen appears to be that
I put up my umbrella.

w. PIERCE DIX on criticism of his refereeing in the Lancashire Cup final, **1881**.

The Commission would urge upon referees and umpires the
necessity of more rigidly enforcing penalties upon players for
breaches of the rules relating to violence and ungentlemanly
conduct, and would also point out to the committees of clubs
the desirability of using their utmost endeavours to prevent and
discountenance all hostile and improper demonstrations against
the players on the part of spectators.

FOOTBALL COMMISSION (Nottingham) edict, November **1888** – the first referees'
clampdown?

> To 'referee'! To regulate the game,
> To earn expenses and a guinea fee!
> Yes! There is great attraction in the name
>   of Referee.
> Yet troublous times might be in store for me,
> Did I allow the visitors a claim!
> A brickbat in the eye or damaged knee,
> Enough to make me permanently lame,
> On second thoughts, then I decline to be –
> (Although, of course, I thank you all the
> same)
>   – A Referee.

ANONYMOUS, *c.* **1890s**.

There was a chap who couldn't run
Whose playing days were long since
done;
And consequently he was free
To rule the game as referee.

A referee can't be too old
While he has strength to take the gold;
Perhaps he cannot run or see
But all the same he'll referee.

J. H. JONES from poem, 'The Age of Referees', *c.* **1900**.

No matter how hard I tried, things happened which I didn't see.
It was not rough play, but things like offside, and before long the
crowd was cat-calling and shouting, 'Get back to Halifax.'

ARTHUR ELLIS, Halifax referee, in *Refereeing Round the World*, **1954**.

The day before the match I received a surprising telephone call
asking me to find two linesmen to take with me to Scotland. They
had forgotten to appoint any!

ARTHUR ELLIS on first round of the European Cup, Hibernian *v.* Rot-Weiss, **1955**.

Ellis is the official who, ignoring my remarks of 'terrible decision'
several times during a match, waited till I had missed an open
goal, then ran past saying 'terrible shot'.

LEN SHACKLETON, in *Clown Prince of Soccer*, **1955**.

After the match an official asked for two of my players to take a
dope test. I offered him the referee.

TOMMY DOCHERTY after 5–1 defeat by Brighton has relegated Wolves to the Third
Division, **1985**.

Bloody English referees.

BERT TRAUTMANN, Manchester City's German goalkeeper, after being sent off *v.*
West Ham, **1962**.

Referees should arrive by the back door and leave by the back door.

ALAN HARDAKER, Football League secretary.

The trouble with referees is that they know the rules but they don't know the game.

BILL SHANKLY during referees' clampdown, **1971**.

People say we've got the best referees in the world – I shudder to think what the rest are like.

MANCHESTER UNITED DEFENDER, **1973**.

Perhaps the natural authority that Englishmen tend to assume over others has a lot to do with their success in this field.

JIMMY HILL in *Striking for Soccer*, **1961**.

The basic training of referees is appalling. When I started as a referee, they tested my eyesight by getting me to stand at one end of a small room, facing a Bukta wall chart showing red, yellow and blue football kits. Some guy pointed to one shirt and said 'What colour's that?' I replied 'Red' and he said 'You're in.'

GORDON HILL, Football League referee, in *Give a Little Whistle*, **1975**.

Most referees see everything that goes on; a good ref is one that doesn't chicken out. A good ref is the one who'll give a penalty at Anfield against Liverpool.

DAVID CROSS, Coventry City striker, in Gordon Hill, *Give a Little Whistle*, **1975**.

I've been booked now over fifty times, but never for fouling, always for dissent. I've seen players really go in to hurt people, and the referee does nothing. I haven't got a good word for any of them. I don't think they control this kind of tackling nearly enough. The newspapers say they've clamped down on it, but they haven't really.

STAN BOWLES, QPR and England midfield player, **1976**.

I got the impression that few toilets were used more than those in the referee's room.

JACK TAYLOR, World Cup referee, in *World Soccer Referee*, **1976**.

Match Officials are the only guys who can rob you and then get a police escort out of the stadium.

RON BOLTON, Cleveland Browns American Footballer, **1978**.

If you painted one of our soccer balls orange and threw it to a linesman, he'd probably try to peel it.

JIMMY GABRIEL, Seattle Sounders' coach, **1979**.

I hate Saturdays off. I'd rather take a village game than stay at home. It's that sort of gut feeling that distinguishes the referee from all the other breeds. Money doesn't come into it. If it did I would never have blown a whistle in my life.

PAT PARTRIDGE, League referee, in *Oh, Ref!*, **1979**.

'Referee, what would you do if I called you a bastard?' one player inquired politely. 'I'd send you off,' I replied. 'What would you do if I thought you were a bastard?' was the next question. 'There's not a lot I could do,' I answered. 'In that case, ref, I think you're a bastard,' he said, turning smartly on his heel.

PAT PARTRIDGE in *Oh, Ref!*, **1979**.

I've been one of the victims of the referee's get-tough policies. Their new approach is a joke and has affected my game.

IAN WOOD, Aldershot defender, retiring at the age of twenty-five in **1982** to become . . . a butcher.

He drives you spare sometimes. . .with Clive you are just playing to one man's rules and you don't know what's happening.

GRAHAM TAYLOR, Watford manager, on Clive 'The Book' Thomas, **1982**.

It's getting to the stage where we hate them and they dislike us.

KENNY SANSOM, Arsenal and England left-back, on referees, **1983**.

There's no rapport with referees these days. If you say anything you get booked, and if you don't they send you off for dumb insolence.

JACK CHARLTON, **1983**.

8
Ladies in Waiting

A bad wife, of course, can ruin a player's career. . .just as she would ruin any man's career! A good wife is a blessing from above, constituting, as she does, the perfect sheet-anchor for a young athlete to tie himself to.

TOM FINNEY, Preston and England forward, in *Finney on Football*, **1958**.

You can have no idea what it's like in the League. Every big game and there they all sit in a group. . .the wives. The bitchiness and backbiting that go on would turn your stomach. You'd think it was Miss World. You should hear them when things are going wrong. Every girl can only see her own man's skill. . .and the faults in all the others.

JUDITH HURST, wife of Geoff, in Brian James, *Journey to Wembley*, **1977**.

Better to marry an over-priced star than a free transfer I always say.

JUDITH HURST quoting bitchy banter among wives.

The Italians are a gayer set of lads who love life, and their girl-friends. Especially their girlfriends – if one is to judge from the many conversations I've overheard on football grounds all over the country. They think the English boys are slightly mad putting sport before the ladies.

EDDIE FIRMANI, on his transfer from Charlton to Sampdoria, in *Football with the Millionaires*, **1960**.

He [the Italian footballer] gets mobbed by the girls with all the zest which seems to follow Johnny Ray around the world, and there are times when these young ladies become a nuisance and ought to be spanked and sent home to bed.

EDDIE FIRMANI in *Football with the Millionaires*, **1960**.

Nearly 800 girl readers wrote in during the close season to say that Gerry Bridgwood of Stoke City was the most attractive man in League football.

FOOTBALL LEAGUE REVIEW, **1967**.

I like to express myself through dance. I like to see people feel what I feel when they watch my movements. My message is mostly love.

VONCEIL BAKER, Dallas Cowboys cheerleader, **1971**.

Basically, he [Bill Nicholson] doesn't think women have any place in football. I never saw him play for Spurs and I'm not allowed to go and see them now. I feel an outsider really, as if I was a member of the opposition.

GRACE NICHOLSON, wife of then Spurs manager, in Hunter Davies, *The Glory Game*, **1972**.

Of course I didn't take my wife to see Rochdale as an anniversary present. It was her birthday. Would I have got married during the football season? And anyway it wasn't Rochdale, it was Rochdale Reserves.

BILL SHANKLY.

When I lose I've got to talk about it. Some keep it inside them. I go home and relive it with the wife. She just nods and says yes or no.

NORMAN HUNTER, Leeds and England defender, **1973**.

Women's soccer arouses unhealthy excitement among some spectators. . .and is harmful to a woman's organism in that it may cause damage to sexual functions.

SOVIET GOVERNMENT REPORT, **1973**.

I used to stand up and glare around when fans were giving Geoff stick and they all used to shout: 'Wasn't me, Mrs Hurstie. . .wasn't me'. Geoff told me again and again to hold my tongue. Norman Hunter's mum used to lash out with her handbag when people booed her Norman.

JUDITH HURST, wife of Geoff, in Brian James, *Journey to Wembley*, **1977**.

It is as plain as can be that football does not come within the Equal Opportunities Act.

LORD DENNING, Master of the Rolls, on the Appeal Court's refusal to overturn decision to stop twelve-year-old Theresa Bennett playing for a boys' club in the **1970s**.

Isn't one of the main features of football-match attendance still that it enables men to get away from nagging wives?

FRANK BURROWS, Portsmouth manager, **1981**.

I recently met Jimmy Hill who argues for football as a family game. When I actually spoke to him, his reaction was polite but uninterested.

JILL TOWNSEND, girlfriend of musician Alan Price (then a Fulham director), **1981**.

Do you know that the thing managers dread is a player's wife becoming pregnant? It affects their game. . .a player gets worried and he loses form. A woman manager might be in a position to set his mind at rest about things and a whole host of other domestic difficulties like bust-ups with girlfriends.

JILL TOWNSEND, **1981**.

I was conscious of a red-headed woman with her husband leaning over the fence to my right. She shrieked at me: 'Not that way, *that* way!' It's bad enough to be told what to do on the field by men without having women butting in; so on the spur of the moment I turned and said to her: 'Don't hen-peck me, hen-peck him!'

JIMMY HILL in *Striking for Soccer*, **1961**.

John Bond has blackened my name with his insinuations about the private lives of football managers. Both my wives are upset.

MALCOLM ALLISON, **1983**.

He leaves pregnant women on every street corner.

JOSEPH-LUIS NUNEZ, Barcelona president, on the Real Madrid player Juanito, **1982**. The remark caused a defamation suit.

I hope they will be waiting for me at the airport where I will attempt to satisfy them.

SERGINHO of Brazil on being voted, by Brazilian women, 'Most attractive player' in **1982** World Cup.

My wife has been magic about it.

JOHN BOND, when the story of his affair with a Manchester City employee broke two days after his resignation as manager, **1983**.

We hope to revive the old tradition of the husband going to football on Christmas day, while the wives cook the turkey.

ERIC WHITE, Brentford official, **1983**.

You can only play this game one time. If they (wives and girl-friends) can't wait, tell them to take a cold shower.

MIKE DITKA, Chicago Bears American Football coach, announcing pre-Super Bowl curfew, **1986**.

My idea of relaxation: Going somewhere away from the wife.

TERRY FENWICK, QPR captain, in *Match* magazine, **1986**.

A lot of beautiful girls may be made available to you before the game. Such traps are aimed at destabilising you. You are going to war and must be on the lookout for all kinds of weapons.

KING MTETWA, Swaziland Home Affairs minister, to Highlanders FC before game in Lesotho, **1985**.

9

We are the People

To go to the match was to escape from the dark of despondency into the light of combat. Here, by association with the home team, positive identity could be claimed in muscle and goals. To win was personal success, to lose another clout from life. Football was not so much an opiate of the masses as a flag run up against the gaffer bolting his gates and the landlord armed with his bailiffs.

ARTHUR HOPCRAFT, *The Football Man*, **1968**.

A northern horde of uncouth garb and strange oaths.

Pall Mall Gazette on Blackburn Rovers fans in London for the **1884** Cup final.

That Association Football is becoming notorious for scenes and disgraceful exhibitions of ruffianism. That the rabble will soon make it impossible for law-abiding citizens to attend matches.

Scottish Athletic Journal article headed 'Things Worth Knowing', 27 September **1887**.

I venture to suggest the turn has come of the public who bring the grist to the mill. Why not covered accommodation for spectators, dry ground to stand on, and a reduced admission if possible. The profits will stand it. Many a wreath has been purchased by standing on wet ground on Saturday afternoons.

LETTER signed A.M.H., *Birmingham Mail*, March **1905**.

Though they were all very excited they conducted themselves with as much decorum as if they had been millionaires, except that they showed more impatience over the slowness of the train.

Pastime magazine's description of 1000 Luton supporters arriving at King's Cross en route for Millwall, **1905**.

A very large proportion of the Crystal Palace crowd (for the FA Cup final) is composed of provincials who travel, many of them, by night excursions from various grimy manufacturing centres in the North and Midlands, being dumped down in the heart of London when the streets are almost deserted.

PICKFORD and GIBSON, **1906**.

There is no real local interest to excuse the frenzy of the mob, since the players come from all over the kingdom, and may change their clubs each season.

C. B. Fry's Magazine on crowd trouble, **1906**.

If they knew more about football than we do, there would be 50,000 players and twenty-two spectators.

BILL McCRACKEN, Newcastle and Northern Ireland player, after being barracked, **1911**.

There was no occasion for the trains to be timed so early for the last of them to reach the destination an hour and three-quarters before the match was due to start which is an unnecessarily long spell and is not in the interest of temperance.

Oldham Chronicle explaining Athletic's lack of support in the FA Cup semi-final *v*. Aston Villa, **1913**.

Generally he is short of stature, anaemic-looking, with a head too big to suggest it contains only brains, a high shrieking voice, reminiscent of a rusty saw in quick staccato action. He is blind to every good move initiated by the Swansea Town players, but his attention to a faulty clearance or badly placed pass is microscopic.

'CYGNET' on the barrackers of Vetch Field in the local *Sporting News*, **1921**.

All the fun seems to have gone out of football today. Once Derby were 3–0 down against Oldham and diving into the Second Division. I'd fallen back to help our defence and someone played the ball out of our penalty area to me. I took it up and was just looking up to see what to do when a voice in the crowd shouted: 'Shoot, George!' Then a voice boomed back from another section of the terracing; 'Why pick on George? Why not shoot the bloody lot?'

GEORGE THORNEWELL, Derby County and England winger, 1919–27, in Andrew Ward and Anton Rippon, *The Derby County Story*, **1983**.

You folks may be rightly proud of your title 'Football's Fairest Crowd', but for my part I would like to see not a little but a lot more partisanship in favour of Chelsea. All too many people come to Stamford Bridge to see a football match – instead of to cheer Chelsea.

TED DRAKE, Chelsea manager, in club programme, August **1952**.

There are times when, as a guest in the boardroom of some mighty First League club, I find that the Third Division results are not read out – they stop at the Second Division. Then it is that I face superior smiles or the loud laughs and ask, with my heart in my mouth, anxious as ever, 'How did Reading get on?'

JOHN ARLOTT from *Concerning Soccer*, **1950**. Arlott cycled sixteen miles each way from his Hampshire home to support Reading as a boy.

A policeman phoned me at home the other week. Friday night again. He'd caught a dozen courting couples in the stand and asked me what to do with them. I told him to fix the bloody fence and board 'em in. Best gate of the season it would've been.

FRED WESTGARTH, Hartlepool United's manager, in **1950s**.

I got the ball in the middle of the field and a voice out of the centre stand shouted out, 'Give it to Taylor.' So I gave it to Taylor. Five minutes afterwards, I got the ball again in the middle of the field and the same voice shouted, 'Give it to Matthews.' So I gave it to Matthews. A couple of minutes later, I got the ball again, but this time there were three Arsenal players around me so I looked up at the stand and the voice came back, 'Use your own discretion.'

STAN MORTENSEN, Blackpool and England player, in Robin Daniels, *Blackpool Football*, **1972**.

On Saturday evenings the Barnsley streets became a sea of 'Green 'Uns' as the fanatics read the *Sheffield Star* reports. They met their wives and, depending on their mood after the match, took a night on the town, perhaps a meal at the bus-station cafe, or a visit to one of the eight cinemas or a dance-hall. Occasionally a man could be seen reading the 'Green 'Un' behind his partner's back as they waltzed.

ALISTER & WARD in *Barnsley – A Study in Football, 1953–59*.

To me, the youngsters who wait patiently – often for hours in the rain – with a well-kept autograph book are to be commended. Firstly they have adopted a hobby which does nobody any harm. Secondly they are taking an interest in football – how much better than those who a short time ago were concerned in the 'Rock 'n' Roll Riots'.

BILLY WRIGHT, Wolves and England captain, in *Football is my Passport*, **1959**.

Chants rather than just plain cheering are much more popular on the Continent. If the fans in Britain kept to their 'Two, four, six, eight. Who do we appreciate?' or their 'One, two, three, four. Who is it that we are for?' they would come into line with the Continental fan, who likes chanting and applauding rather than what he might call the 'undisciplined' cheering of the British.

JOHN CHARLES, Juventus and Wales, in *The Gentle Giant*, **1962**.

It's gone now, mainly because of hooliganism. I wouldn't dare walk about now, in my old outfit, in another town. They'd be after me, wouldn't they? Around 1963, I could feel that some spectators were getting out of hand.

SYD BEVERS, leader of the 'Atomic Boys', a group of Blackpool fans who went to matches in fancy-dress in the **1950s**.

As a boy I genuinely believed in the man who never ate bacon because its red and white stripes reminded him of Sheffield United – indeed in my blue and white Wednesday heart I applauded and supported his loyalty.

ROY HATTERSLEY MP in *Goodbye to Yorkshire*, **1976**.

Most people are in a factory from nine till five. Their job may be to turn out 263 little circles. At the end of the week they're three short and somebody has a go at them. On Saturday afternoons they deserve something to go and shout at.

RODNEY MARSH, **1967**.

They tend to start off with things like 'Dear Stupid' or 'Dear Big Head'. One man wrote to me, beginning 'Dear Alfie Boy'.

SIR ALF RAMSEY on letters he received after internationals, in Arthur Hopcraft, *The Football Man*, **1968**.

The Spurs fans, marching and shouting their way back to the station, banged on the windows of the coach as it threaded its way back through the crowds. 'Go on, smash the town up,' said Cyril [Knowles], encouraging them.

HUNTER DAVIES, *The Glory Game*, **1972**.

The club call us hooligans, but who'd cheer them if we didn't come? You have to stand there and take it when Spurs are losing and the others are jeering at you. It's not easy. We support them everywhere and we get no thanks.

SPURS FAN quoted in Hunter Davies, *The Glory Game*, **1972**.

I'd like to kill all the Arsenal players and then burn the stand down.

SPURS FAN, in Hunter Davies, *The Glory Game*, **1972**.

Their support can be an embarrassment sometimes, but I'd rather have them as an embarrassment than not at all.

TOMMY DOCHERTY on Manchester United fans, **1974**.

The image of the British gentleman along the Belgian coast has given way to one of truculent youths, throwing cobblestones and wielding sticks.

JEAN-MARIE BERKVENS, Belgian attorney, on rioting Manchester United fans at Ostend, **1974**.

The Belgians have got the answer – jail them without trial, put them in a dungeon and half-starve them. That would cure Britain's soccer hooligans.

JOHN MORAN, Manchester United fan jailed in Ostend, **1974**.

The violence was sickening. The only answer is for decent supporters – and they are in the majority – to become vigilantes on the terraces. A few thumps on the nose would soon stop these silly youngsters.

ALEC STOCK, Fulham manager, **1975**.

I was bloody scared. Who wouldn't be, surrounded by wild animals like that?

PC TED CARRINGTON after duty at Spurs *v*. Chelsea match, **1975**.

Society's values are such that one man's hooligan is another man's OBE.

EAMON DUNPHY, **1975**.

Sunderland's Barry Venison once autographed my head.

My mother once bumped into Oxford's Gary Briggs in Tescos.

The best man at my grandfather's wedding was the father-in-law of Middlesbrough manager Willie Maddren.

LETTERS from readers to 'Claim To Fame' in *Match* magazine, **1985**.

My favourite [letter received] is one which said 'You. . . Smith. . .Jones and Heighway had better keep looking over your shoulder. You are going to get your dews.'

EMLYN HUGHES, in Brian James, *Journey to Wembley*, **1977**.

Apparently they couldn't find one decent Millwall supporter.

DENIS HOWELL MP, Minister for Sport, complaining about an 'irresponsible' and 'unbalanced' edition of BBC1's 'Panorama' on football hooliganism, **1977**.

Really good Millwall supporters, right, they can't stand their club being slagged down you know, and it all wells up, you know, and you just feel like hitting someone.

MILLWALL FANS in Roger Ingham *et al.*, *Football Hooliganism: The Wider Context*, **1978**.

It's bad enough to have to go and watch Bristol City without having things stolen.

JUDGE DESMOND VOWDEN QC, sentencing man who stole from a City fan's car, **1984**.

Q. What will you do when Christ comes to lead us again?
A. Move St John to inside-right.

CHURCH SIGN and answering graffiti on Merseyside in the **1960s**.

After three games this season, I know my club Birmingham City are going to be relegated. Is this a record?

LETTER to *Sunday People*, **1977**.

Just about the only point worth remembering about Port Vale's match with Hereford on Monday evening was the fact that the attendance figure, 2744, is a perfect cube, 14 × 14 × 14.

DISILLUSIONED SUPPORTER, Congleton, letter to *Stoke Evening Sentinel*, **1979**.

Even Altrincham's kit was smarter.

LETTER to *Birmingham Post* from Birmingham fan after Cup defeat by the non-Leaguers, **1986**.

You lose some, you draw some.

JASPER CARROTT, comedian, on supporting Birmingham City, **1978**.

One thing that does anger me is to see Rangers or Celtic fanatics getting all steamed up in the name of religion when most of them have never been near a church or chapel for years.

DEREK JOHNSTONE, Glasgow Rangers and Scotland player, in *Rangers – My Team*, **1979**.

With a small crowd like we had today, you can hear them all shouting. It's not very pleasant but I can understand them. It's their club, after all.

BOBBY CAMPBELL, Fulham manager, after home defeat by Oxford, **1980**.

SUPPORTER: A fiver on Celtic tae beat Arsenal.
WORKER: Sorry sir, we don't take bets on friendlies.
SUPPORTER: Celtic dinnae play friendlies. . . .

EXCHANGE in Islington bookmaker's before Arsenal *v*. Celtic testimonial, **1980**.

Players have a duty to avoid actions which can inflame their supporters on the terraces. We have a right to expect these highly paid young men to set an example to those who watch them.

RT. HON. WILLIAM WHITELAW MP, Home Secretary, at Police Superintendents' Association Conference, **1980**.

The most violent offenders should be flogged in front of the main stand before the start of a home game. I feel so strongly on this matter, I'd volunteer to do the whipping myself.

ALLAN CLARKE, Leeds manager, **1980**.

I know it sounds drastic, but the only way to deal with hooligans is to shoot them. That'll stop 'em.

BOBBY ROBERTS, Colchester manager, **1980**.

I met these football fans smoking in a non-smoker on the railway, so I said: 'Put it out. . .put it out. . .put it out.' And they did. I think they're far less dangerous than dogs.

BARBARA WOODHOUSE, dog trainer, **1980**.

There are more hooligans in the House of Commons than at a football match.

BRIAN CLOUGH, **1980**.

I wish they would all be put on a boat and dropped in the ocean. We are ashamed of people like this. The Italians must think we are idiots.

RON GREENWOOD, England manager, after riots in Turin, **1980**.

There is no doubt that Britian is a country rich in culture and tradition but its soccer envoys abroad are worse than the barbarous hordes headed by Attila.

SPANISH NEWSPAPER editorial after fights at Castilla-West Ham game, **1980**.

The offenders should be apprehended and shipped back to England in chains.

AUSTRALIAN NEWSPAPER editorial after trouble involving English expatriates at World Youth Cup game in Sydney, **1982**.

The Swiss police are accustomed to dealing sensibly with political and student demonstrations. We have special units to combat terrorists at our airports. But the behaviour of the English fans was outside our experience.

DR MARKUS MOHLER, Basle Chief of Police, after Switzerland *v*. England game, **1981**.

As a word of caution, I would only say that methods of controlling fans in countries such as Spain are in stark contrast to our own.

NEIL MACFARLANE MP, Minister for Sport, **1981**.

Their ability to smuggle drink into matches makes Papillon look like a learner.

SCOTTISH POLICE FEDERATION spokesman, **1981**.

There's a new breed of flash young executives who think they've got the right to call to account anybody in the world.

RON GREENWOOD after the Wembley crowd had booed his side against Spain, **1981**.

It's a pity your hooligans aren't coming. We like your hooligans. We think you have the best hooligans in Europe.

GREEK TAXI DRIVER on being informed that not many England fans were visiting Salonika, **1982**.

A moral panic about hooliganism led many to think in terms of appealing to a more affluent consumer. They saw the way ahead in terms of all-seater stadiums, executive boxes complete with colour TV and cocktail cabinet and the mythical 'family audience'. . . . The fall-off in crowds during the 1970s has been mainly among working-class supporters. This is hardly surprising when most clubs seem bent on ignoring the terrace fans to concentrate on their new executive box-dwellers.

GARRY WHANNEL, *Blowing the Whistle: the Politics of Sport*, **1983**.

They came for warfare, to cause trouble and fight. It's been said that they're a small minority. They are not. There were nearly 1700 of them and nearly all of them were at it.

BERT MILLICHIP, FA chairman, on England fans in Luxembourg, **1983**.

Tottenham's supporters were exemplary, the sort of guests we always like to have here.

BAYERN MUNICH official, **1983**.

We can no longer call these people hooligans. It is terrorism.

JOOP VAN DER REIJDEN, Dutch Minister of Culture, after Spurs' visit to Feyenoord, **1983**.

There are two league tables these days, one for the club matches and the other for the supporters – who ran, when and from whom. And this second league is rooted in lower working-class standards of masculine aggression.

JOHN WILLIAMS, Leicester University sociologist, **1983**.

I've spent six years watching that b— Walker and then he goes and scores two goals against us.

JOHN LEFTLEY, Chelsea fan arrested for trying to punch club's former winger Clive Walker of Sunderland, **1985**.

You must have some sort of deterrent and the first thing I would advocate for these people is the birch. You don't stroke a wild dog, you blow his brains out.

RON SAUNDERS, Birmingham manager, after crowd violence had disrupted an FA Cup tie against West Ham, **1984**.

We don't normally have any police at our matches, unless one happens to wander up on his bike.

SALISBURY TOWN SECRETARY, on hearing his club had drawn Millwall in the FA Cup, **1979**.

I just wish there were 10,000 more in the ground chanting for my blood.

LEN WALKER, Aldershot manager, on demonstration by fifty fans after home defeat by Hartlepool, **1983**.

We were disappointed we couldn't play on Saturday because we had supporters travelling from all over the country. There was one coming from London, one from Newcastle, one from Brighton. . . .

DAVID KILPATRICK, Rochdale chairman, on the postponement of FA Cup tie at Manchester United, **1986**.

We must be the only team in the Football League who would rather play away from home. On other grounds you can build up quite a rapport with the opposing supporters. At Hartlepool it's plain bloody murder.

PHIL BROWN, Hartlepool captain, **1983**.

It may have been an awful night, but the meat and potato pies were brill.

'AWAY TRAVELLER' in the Crewe Alexandra Supporters' Association newsletter, on a visit to Halifax, **1983**.

The Spion Kop at Liverpool is famous, as certain football reporters have discovered when an ill-chosen word in their writings has brought upon their heads a storm of abuse from 'behind the goal'. That Anfield Spion Kop is one of Liverpool Football Club's prized possessions, and in all seriousness, I am certain matches have been won through the vocal efforts of its regular patrons.

MATT BUSBY, ex-Liverpool player, in *My Story*, **1957**.

We all agree, Tiswas is better than Swapshop.

THE KOP during dull passage in Liverpool *v.* Bury FA Cup tie, **1980**.

Sing when you're bevvied, you only sing when you're bevvied.

THE KOP taunting Aberdeen fans during European Cup match at Anfield, **1980**.

He's Ireland's No. 1. . .

THE KOP to Gary Bailey after Manchester United keeper's fumble had presented Irish with a goal *v*. England, **1985**.

> Come along the Rangers
> Buckle up your belts
> You'll mebbe beat the Hearts
> But you'll never beat the Celts.

CELTIC fans' song.

> Follow, follow, we will follow Rangers
> Anywhere, everywhere, we will follow on.

RANGERS fans' song.

Who are the people?
We arra people!

RANGERS fans' call-response chant.

> Glory, glory hallelujah!
> Glory, glory hallelujah!
> And the Spurs go marching on, on, on.

SPURS fans' song. Arsenal supporters try to drown the end with 'out, out, out'.

> I'm forever blowing bubbles
> Pretty bubbles in the air
> They fly so high
> They reach the sky
> Then like West Ham
> They fade and die.

WEST HAM fans' song, as corrupted by rival supporters.

> Land of smoke and glory
> Home of Stoke City
> Higher, higher and higher
> On to victory.

STOKE fans' song.

> What are we living for?
> To see Stoke City in Division Four.

PORT VALE fans' song to tune of Kinks' 'Dead End Street'.

> Where 'ast tha bin since ah saw thee?
> At Ell-and Road baht'at.

LEEDS fans' song from **1960s**, to tune of 'Ilkley Moor'.

> Jingle bells, jingle bells, jingle all the way
> Oh what fun it is to see United win away.

MANCHESTER UNITED fans' song.

> There is a circus in the town, in the town,
> With Joe Hayes as chief clown, chief clown,
> There's Bill Leivers there and Colin Barlow too
> They are the clowns who play in blue, play in blue.
>
> Chorus   In the League you can nearly always spot 'em
> Because they're always on the bottom,
> They are the clowns who play in blue, play in blue.

MANCHESTER UNITED fans' song on Manchester City, early **1960s**, to tune of 'There is a Tavern in the Town'.

> Six foot two, eyes of blue
> Big Jim Holton's after you.

MANCHESTER UNITED fans' song, **1974**.

> Let 'em come, let 'em come, let 'em come,
> Let 'em all come dahn to the Den!

MILLWALL record played before home matches.

I never felt more like singing the Blues
Wednesday win, United lose!

SHEFFIELD WEDNESDAY fans' song.

We are the boys in red and white
We love to sing and we love to fight.

FANS' song to tune of 'Let's Dance'.

Peter Shilton, Peter Shilton, does your missus know you're here?

ARSENAL NORTH BANK to Nottingham Forest goalkeeper after revelation that he
had been caught in a compromising position late at night, **1980**.

Steve Foster, Steve Foster
What a difference you have made.

MANCHESTER UNITED fans' song at Wembley Cup final replay, **1984**. Brighton
captain Foster didn't play in the first match which ended 2–2. United won the
replay 4–0.

Jesus saves, but Pancho nets the rebound.

MANCHESTER UNITED fans' banner at **1977** FA Cup final *v*. Liverpool. Pancho was
Stuart Pearson. Keegan and Dalglish have also figured in similar claims.

Maggie isn't the only one with Crooks at No. 11.

SPURS banner at civic reception after FA Cup victory, **1981**.

Devonshire's the cream, Rice is the pudding.

WEST HAM banner at FA Cup final, **1980**.

Communism *v*. Alcoholism.

SCOTTISH banner at Soviet Union *v*. Scotland World Cup match, **1982**.

Don't worry lads. Ally MacLeod's in Blackpool.

SCOTTISH banner in Seville, **1982**.

No Valley, No Validity.

CHARLTON banner at last match before move to Crystal Palace, **1985**.

The Giro Cup final.

MERSEYSIDE fan on Liverpool *v*. Everton Milk Cup final, **1984**.

They should make Leeds play all their away matches at home.

BILLY HAMILTON, Oxford striker, after riot by visiting Leeds fans, **1984**.

What comes next – water cannon, guards, tanks, and consultant undertakers to ferry away the dead?

SIMON TURNEY, Greater London Council, on Chelsea's proposed electric fence, **1985**.

If somebody is celebrating it means we still have much to learn.

GIORGIO CARDETTI, Mayor of Turin, after Juventus's win following Heysel deaths, **1985**.

10
They Also Serve

I never go to bed until I know where every player is when we're on tour. I'm not a spy nor a headmaster, but I do care about my players and their health.

VERNON EDWARDS, England team doctor, **1983**.

We've found out from this psychiatrist that players who are friends pass to each other more.

MALCOLM ALLISON, **1973**.

Always in uniform, fraying in one or two places, and shoes in need of a quick polish. Face like a bag of chisels, moustache an essential part of the make-up in order to twitch as you approach him.

FRED EYRE, former player with twenty League and non-League teams, on club commissionaires in *Another Breath of Fred Eyre*, **1982**.

Frank Lord is coming with Plymouth Argyle next week. So make sure you don't let him in. Then you can tell all your mates at work that one week you didn't let a 'sir' in, and the next week you didn't let a 'lord' in! Now kindly step aside will you, I've got to get changed.

NORMAN BODELL, Crewe Alexandra player of **1960s**, to recalcitrant doorman who was barring his way, announcing that he had refused admission to Sir Stanley Rous the previous week.

My mind goes back to the 'glory days' at the club, when it was arranged for a certain photographer to photograph me with the players. While waiting for the training session to end he tried to persuade me to wear shorts and jersey and boots. I naturally refused and, when the players became available, he asked them to try and persuade me to get changed. Imagine my joy when one of the senior players remarked, 'Mr Jackson is our chaplain, not our mascot.'

REVEREND JOHN JACKSON, chaplain to Leeds United, in the Methodist Church Home Mission Report, **1984**.

With the dominance of television, the influence of sponsors, the interference of manufacturers, public-relations officers and entrepreneurs, I see no future for sport at top level. It is not too alarming a glimpse into the future to see professional football playing to empty stadia for the benefit of TV and the football pools.

SIR DENIS FOLLOWS, chairman of the British Olympic Association, **1983**.

We are pulling out because FADS is an upright and clean company. That is something which can no longer be said about soccer. It is a sick sport. We would rather sponsor netball.

MALCOLM STANLEY, managing director of FADS, the decorating retailers, ending deal with Charlton, **1982**.

Sponsors! They'll be wanting to pick the team next.

BOB PAISLEY, **1981**.

The first half of this match was so bad that at half-time the sponsors asked for their ball back.

LEN SHACKLETON in press report.

I have even heard of one trainer who claims that the best way to clear up a knee injury is to massage it with oil from the tail of a tiger.

LEN SHACKLETON in *Clown Prince of Soccer*, **1955**.

Agents do nothing for the good of football. I'd like to see them lined up against a wall and machine-gunned. . .some accountants and solicitors with them.

GRAHAM TAYLOR, Watford manager, **1983**.

11

The Fourth Estate

Press

When people first found I reported football, they used to say 'Lucky devil'. I used to think, with a bitter, twisted smile, of the climb up those murderous spiral stairs to the top of the Sheffield United stand, and the half-time quarter meat-pie and tea that tasted like horse-piss. . . . I used to think of all those cracked cups without saucers and those half-daft little members of the Supporters' Club who used to hold their tin tea-pot at the interval and hate us and refuse to serve us if we didn't have the correct half of our press pass.

BILL GRUNDY, journalist, in *Foul!*, **1975**.

Next week Newton Heath have to meet Burnley, and if they both play in their ordinary style it will perhaps create an extra run of business for the undertakers.

Birmingham Daily Gazette on Newton Heath *v*. West Bromwich Albion, **1884**. Newton Heath, later Birmingham City, brought libel damages and won. . .a farthing.

He is to the point with the pen as with the tongue, and calls a football 'the ball'. Such things as 'inflated spheres', 'tegumentary cylinders', and the 'leather globe' he leaves to others. . . . He does not deal in superlatives nor is he led to place the football player of momentary eminence on a pedestal.

PICKFORD and GIBSON, **1906**, on J. J. Bentley, 'Doyen of Journalists', ex-Bolton secretary, FA vice-president and League president.

One or two Glasgow papers used to employ pigeons, and a few country papers still do; but the pigeon is a slow, clumsy and uncertain messenger. Practically all the up-to-date papers now use a telephone for local reports.

PICKFORD and GIBSON, **1906**.

Although I'm only human and do not always agree with sentiments expressed by writers, I'm wise enough, I hope, to appreciate that the spectator sees more of a match than a player, and I can often learn a good deal by studying some of the reporters' comments.

ALF RAMSEY, the player.

No club official likes the type of correspondent who constantly seeks information from players by visiting their homes or ringing them up on the telephone at all hours. These are the hole-and-corner methods of the few to which we take exception.

BOB LORD, Burnley chairman, on why he had barred journalists from the press-box, in *My Fight for Football*, **1963**.

Queen in brawl at Palace.

Guardian headline, **1970**. Crystal Palace had a forward called Gerry Queen.

Nobody can watch a football match and write it down. They can write about certain things that happened in the game, the illusions that affected them. But when you consider that there are twenty-two players on the pitch, with twenty of them running about, and they cover between three and six miles, and they're in competition with each other – and there's one man going to write about what happens – he gets misled. The shrewdest players never take any notice whatsoever of good press or bad press.

MALCOLM ALLISON, **1971**.

The End of the World!

Sun headline after England failed to beat Poland to qualify for World Cup finals, **1973**.

I did some commentaries up in Yorkshire, but I didn't really enjoy it. You'd criticize the home team, and they didn't like that. They'd get 30,000 people from Leeds writing in and complaining. I'd much rather have done something afterwards, analysed it; not just saying 'that's a bad pass', but stopping it, explaining *why* it was a bad pass. But there's no time to explain anything, to educate.

DANNY BLANCHFLOWER, **1972**.

He's fairly respectful most of the time; then every so often he gives somebody a kick in the crutch, and I think 'Good old Danny'.

ARTHUR ROWE on Blanchflower the journalist, **1975**.

Savages! Animals!

Daily Mirror headline after weekend of terrace violence, **1975**.

I've no confidence in any soccer reporter.

STEVE HEIGHWAY, Liverpool forward, **1970s**.

Reporters can make or break footballers. The reverse can rarely be said.

MALCOLM MACDONALD, England striker, **1970s**.

Reporters want a quick answer to something I might need all Saturday night and all Sunday to get somewhere near.

HOWARD WILKINSON, Sheffield Wednesday manager, **1983**.

I have to make a living just like you. I happen to make mine in a nice way – you happen to make yours in a nasty way.

SIR ALF RAMSEY to journalists in **1973**.

With a few rare exceptions. . .sportswriters are a kind of rude and brainless subculture of fascist drunks whose only real function is to publicize and sell whatever the sports editor sends them out to cover.

HUNTER S. THOMPSON, in 'Fear and Loathing at the Super Bowl', *Rolling Stone*, **1973**.

People don't know what they're seeing, reporters don't know what's happening. I throw a pass that's intercepted and people blame me when it was the fault of someone who wasn't where he should have been. I throw a touchdown pass and I get the credit when it was underthrown and only a great catch made the play.

JOE NAMATH, New York Jets quarterback, on the American Football media, **1970**.

I took the paper and scanned the article, eyes acutely sensitive to the peculiar shape of my name. It was all very silly and seeing myself quoted incorrectly in print embarrassed me. Sportswriters were such assholes. They didn't know shit and acted as if they understood a game far more complex in emotion and technical skills than they had the ability to comprehend. They couldn't even transcribe my jokes correctly.

PETER GENT, ex-Dallas cowboys player, in novel, *North Dallas Forty*, **1973**.

They were Rotherham fellers, writing in a Rotherham paper, for other Rotherham fellers, so bugger impartiality.

BILL GRUNDY, journalist, in *Foul!*, **1975**.

Theatre critics and film critics do know what the mechanics of a production are. Most football writers don't. So players tend to despise journalists. On the other hand players are flattered by their attention. Flattered by the idea that this guy has come along especially to write about them. So you have contempt and at the same time a slight awe at seeing your name in print.

EAMON DUNPHY in *Only a Game?*, **1976**.

HANDY PHRASES: *Dejen de torturame, por favor* (Please stop torturing me). *Mi periodico les pagara bien si mi dejen ir* (My newspaper will pay well if you let me go). *Por favor entregan mi cuerpo a mi familia* (Please deliver my body to my family).

NATIONAL UNION OF JOURNALISTS guidelines for reporters at **1978** World Cup in Argentina.

Mr Martinez [referee] was slow to realize that the Dutch invented the clog.

DAVID LACEY in *The Guardian* on the **1978** World Cup match between Holland and Italy.

I don't take any notice of the stick people give me. The press and media have lived off people like myself and they seem to enjoy criticizing without any real reason.

MALCOLM ALLISON, **1979**.

On slow days the Rome papers would send reporters to my house to get my comments on anything. The quotes were always on page one. The Pope, he was on page three.

GIORGIO CHINAGLIA, former Lazio and Italy striker, **1979**.

A lot of people in football don't have much time for the press: they say they're amateurs. But I say to those people, 'Noah built the ark, but the Titanic was built by professionals.'

MALCOLM ALLISON, **1980**.

Arsenal: A Nation Mourns.

Guardian headline after Arsenal's FA Cup defeat at Everton ensured they would not make a fourth successive final appearance, **1981**.

Half an hour? You could shoot Ben Hur in half an hour. You've got 15 seconds.

RON ATKINSON, Manchester United manager, to photographer who asked for 30 minutes with him, **1984**.

I find that if I have a go at them on a one to one basis, very few can take it. They just can't take the criticism they shovel out in bucketfuls.

BOBBY ROBSON on the press, **1985**.

Strictly off the record, no comment.

COLIN MURPHY, Lincoln manager, **1983**.

Not only do they know nothing about football, but if you were to shut them up in a room by themselves they couldn't even write a letter to mother.

CESAR MENOTTI, Argentina's manager, on his country's soccer journalists, **1982**.

Mr Stanley Heathman, married with five children, said that they had never been in doubt they would be liberated. It was just a matter of how and when. He astonished one soldier by asking: 'Can you tell me – have Leeds been relegated?'

POOLED DISPATCH by journalists during Falklands War, **1982**.

Argies Smashed!

Sun headline after Argentina's defeat by Belgium, World Cup **1982**.

Irish frivolity masks both fitness and resolve.

Times headline, World Cup **1982**.

JOURNALIST: Of course, it's all very well playing a sweeper if you're
    Italian, but it's quite a different matter if you're English.
TERRY NEILL: I wouldn't know about that, we're all Irish here.

EXCHANGE at press conference after Arsenal *v.* Southampton FA Cup tie, **1979**.

'What do you think of Brazil?' 'I think he's a great player.'

INTERCHANGE between Brazilian journalist and Kenny Dalglish during **1982** World Cup.

O Nosse Futebol E Como A Nossa Inflacco. . .100% (Our Football is Like Our Inflation. . .100%)

Jornal da Tarde headline after Brazil's win over England, **1981**.

You saw a damned good game of football, but I suppose the media will ignore that and sensationalise a few minutes of crowd trouble.

BERT MILLICHIP, FA chairman, after pitch invasion at Chelsea *v.* Sunderland, Milk Cup semi-final, **1985**.

Television

How many times do you walk past a spare piece of land and see it vacant? – Not a youngster in sight, certainly not one playing football. No, the moment youngsters are freed from their school lessons, they rush home to pick up a few hints on how to handle a gun – from the small-screen monster which seems to be a 'must' in every household. I'm certainly not advocating that television should be banned. I've got one and I enjoy watching various programmes. But this goggle-box has become a drug with many youngsters.

RONNIE CLAYTON, Blackburn Rovers and England player, in *A Slave – to Soccer*, **1960**.

As soon as television completed the circle and we learned that we could sit at home and see the mid-field tussles and the goalmouth scrimmages in the purest detail we allowed science to be our ally.

DR PERCY M. YOUNG on the coming of floodlit football, in *Football Year, 1956*.

There are people on the pitch. . .they think it's all over (*Hurst completes hat-trick*). . .It is now!

KENNETH WOLSTENHOLME, BBC commentator, at the end of World Cup final, **1966**.

Blanchflower's blend of running criticism, boundless compassion and sterling cliché eased the visual ennui.

NEW YORK TIMES television critic on the CBS soccer transmissions, **1968**.

Blanchflower killed us last year, pointing out all the bad things. He was so honest he hurt us. His job was to promote the sport. That's what we were paying him to do.

BILL BERGESCH, general manager of the New York Generals, on Blanchflower's season as an American television commentator.

It was when old ladies who had been coming into my shop for years started talking about sweepers and creating space that I really understood the influence of televison.

JACK TAYLOR, referee, **1974**.

At the ITV Cup final my enjoyment was considerably impaired by an occasional high-pitched whine on my television set. On ringing up to complain I was told it was Alan Ball.

SCOUSE BENNY in *Foul!*, **1975**.

Football on TV on a Sunday afternoon is an entertainment. I have a duty to my employers to present as entertaining a programme as possible – not just for committed football fans, but for the guy in the street and for Mum.

BRIAN MOORE, 'The Big Match' presenter, **1975**.

This isn't the sort of thing we like to see on Match of the Day, or for that matter in football.

JIMMY HILL on Billy Bonds *v.* Terry Yorath altercation, **1975**.

I would say that 90 per cent of the behaviour trouble we have in schools football comes from the influence of television.

KEN ASTON, ex-World Cup referee and primary-school headmaster.

If he can find a ground where he scored a League goal, I'll meet him there.

BRIAN CLOUGH replying to Jimmy Hill's challenge to debate, **1979**.

There! He blew the whistle! Norway has beaten England 2–1 in football and we are the best in the world! It is quite unbelievable – we have beaten England, England the home of the giants! Lord Nelson! Lord Beaverbrook! Sir Winston Churchill! Sir Anthony Eden! Clement Attlee! Henry Cooper! Lady Diana!
   Maggie Thatcher, can you hear me? Maggie Thatcher I have a message for you in your campaigning. We have beaten England in the World Cup! As they say in your language and as they say in the boxing bars around Madison Square Gardens in New York, your boys took a hell of a beating!

BJORGE LILLELIEN, Norwegian television commentator, after Norway's victory over England, **1981**.

I don't think they [Ricoh, the sponsors] will be too happy if we're top of the League and on TV every week, because then we won't be able to wear their name on our shirts.

RICHIE BARKER, Stoke manager, in **1981** before television lifted ban on sponsors' names.

We want football to tell us exactly what they would like in the ideal world and then, I'd assume, we will tell them what they can have.

JOHN BROMLEY, Head of ITV Sport, **1982**.

Well that's the magic of television, isn't it? You hype up the sound a bit, point the cameras where the crowd is thickest, cut out all the boring rubbish, and you've got The Big Match.

TED AYLING, 'The Big Match' director, **1982**.

When the League offered us thirty-one matches 'live', we said: 'Can you deliver?' The answer was: 'Anything can be delivered, so long as the money's right.' I was shattered that they could believe that money is more important than the welfare of the game.

CLIFF MORGAN, BBC Head of Outside Broadcasts, **1983**.

I find it ironical that Brian Clough should call for a total ban on TV soccer after making the kind of money as a member of TV's World Cup panel that would seem a pools win to small clubs.

DEREK DOUGAN, former panel colleague, **1983**.

I'm sure the top clubs would be magnanimous and give some of the money to the small clubs, but it's essential that we keep the lion's share.

DOUGLAS ALEXIOU, Spurs chairman, on the threat of breakaway negotiations with television by the big clubs, **1983**.

The liberties you people take are unbelievable. You TV people seem to think you are entitled to intrude wherever and whenever you want.

RON GREENWOOD, England manager, ordering cameras out of team's HQ before match, **1981**.

There's only one thing better than getting an interview with Ron Greenwood. That's not getting an interview with him.

TONY FRANCIS, ITN sports reporter, **1981**.

It's our policy to show the better side of the game. It's not censorship, it's selectivity.

BOB ABRAHAMS, 'Match of the Day' editor, explaining why the violence in the Birmingham v. Watford FA Cup match, **1984**, had been cut.

I should rather like the Match of the Day theme tune played at my funeral.

CARDINAL BASIL HUME, Newcastle United fan, **1986**.

I don't watch television myself. But my family do and they tell me the most popular programmes are the ones which are full of violence. On that basis football ought to do rather well.

JACK DUNNETT, Football League president, **1985**.

In one sense soccer is like religion. It must be witnessed in the place of worship.

BOB WALL, Arsenal secretary, after 7,483 had watched Scotland *v*. Northern Ireland at Hampden – and 13 million on TV, **1969**.

12
Literary Lions

The sturdie ploughman, lustie, strong and bold,
Overcometh the winter with driving the foote-ball,
Forgetting labour and many a grievous fall.

ALEXANDER BARCLAY in *Fifth Eclogue*, **1508**.

The streets were full of footballs.

SAMUEL PEPYS in his diary, 2 January, **1665**.

Am I so round with you as you with me.
That like a football you do spurn me thus?
You spurn me hence, and he will spurn me hither;
If I last in this service you must case me leather.

WILLIAM SHAKESPEARE in *Comedy of Errors*, **1590**.

OSWALD: I'll not be strucken, my lord.
KENT: Nor tripp'd neither, you base football player. (*Tripping up his heels*).

SHAKESPEARE in *King Lear*, **1608**.

ANTONY: Do we have best them to their beds. What, girl! though grey
Do something mingle with our younger brown, yet ha'we
A brain that nourishes our nerves, and can
Get goal for goal of youth.

SHAKESPEARE in *Antony and Cleopatra*, **1608**.

Like a wild Irish, I'll nere thinke thee dead.
Till I can play at football with thy head.

JOHN WEBSTER in 'The White Devil', **1612**.

How the quoit
Wizz'd from the stripling's arm!
If touched by him,
The inglorious football mounted to the pitch
Of the lark's flight, – or shaped a rainbow curve
Aloft, in prospect of the shouting field.

WILLIAM WORDSWORTH in 'The Excursion', **1814**.

Then strip lads and to it, though sharp be the weather
And if, by mischance, you should happen to fall,
There are worse things in life than a tumble in the heather,
And life itself is but a game of football.

SIR WALTER SCOTT, on the occasion of a match between Ettrick and Selkirk, **1815**.

Twice a week the winter through
Here stood I to keep the goal:
Football then was fighting sorrow
For the young man's soul.

A. E. HOUSMAN, '*A Shropshire Lad*', **1896**.

Then ye returned to your trinkets;
Then ye contented your souls
With the flanelled fools at the wicket
Or the muddied oafs at the goals.

RUDYARD KIPLING in 'The Islanders', **1902**.

Football is all very well as a game for rough girls, but it is hardly
suitable for delicate boys.

OSCAR WILDE.

'But I don't see what football has got to do with being mayor.'
She endeavoured to look like a serious politician. 'You are nothing
but a cuckoo,' Denry pleasantly informed her. 'Football has got
to do with everything.'

ARNOLD BENNETT in *The Card*, **1911**.

'I've lost that £2000 in thirteen years. That is, it's the same as if
I'd been steadily paying three pun' a week out of my own pocket
to provide football matches that you chaps wouldn't take the
trouble to go and see. That's the straight of it! What have I got
for my pains? Nothing but worries and these!' (He pointed to his
grey hairs). . . . 'Me and my co-directors,' he proceeded, with
even tougher raspishness, 'have warned the town again and again
what would happen if the matches weren't better patronised. And
now it's happening, and now it's too late, you want to *do* something! You can't! It's too late. There's only one thing the matter
with first-class football in Bursley,' he concluded, 'and it isn't the
players. It's the public – it's yourselves. You're the most craven
lot of tom-fools that ever a big football club had to do with.'

ARNOLD BENNETT in *The Card*, **1911**.

Rangers would play with the sou'westerly wind, straight towards
the goal behind which Danny stood in eagerness. This was enough
to send a man off his head. Good old Rangers – and to hell with
the Pope.

GEORGE BLAKE in *The Shipbuilders*, **1957**.

Nearly two hours thereafter Danny Shields lived far beyond
himself in a whirling world of passion. Not a man on the terrace
paused to reflect that it was a spectacle cunningly arranged to
draw their shillings or to remember that the twenty-two players
were so many slaves of a commercial system, liable to be bought
and sold like fallen women without any regard to their feelings as
men. The men on the terraces found release from the drabness
of their own industrial degradation.

GEORGE BLAKE, *The Shipbuilders*, **1957**.

To say that these men paid their shillings to watch twenty-two hirelings kick a ball is merely to say that a violin is wood and catgut, that Hamlet is so much paper and ink. For a shilling the Bruddersford United AFC offered you Conflict and Art. . . .

J. B. PRIESTLEY in *The Good Companions*, **1929**.

A man who had missed the last home match of 't 'United' had to enter social life on tiptoe in Bruddersford.

J. B. PRIESTLEY, *The Good Companions*, **1929**.

It turned you into a member of a community, all brothers together for an hour and a half, for not only had you escaped from the clanking machinery of the lesser life, from work, wages, rent, doles, sick pay, insurance cards, nagging wives, ailing children, bad bosses, idle workmen, but you had escaped with most of your mates, and your neighbours, with half the town, and there you were, cheering together, thumping one another on the shoulders, swapping judgements like lords of the earth, having punched your way through a turnstile into another and altogether more special kind of life.

J. B. PRIESTLEY, *The Good Companions*, **1929**.

> When at Thy call my weary feet I turn,
> The gates of paradise are open wide,
> At Goodison I know a man can learn
> Rapture more rich than Anfield can provide.
> In Coulter's skill and Geldard's subtle speed,
> I see displayed in all its bounty
> The power of which the heavens decreed,
> The fall of Sunderland and Derby County.
> The hands of Sagar, Dixie's priceless head,
> Made smooth the path to Wembley till that day
> When Bolton came. Now hopes are fled
> And all is sunk in bottomless dismay,
> And so I watch with heart and temper cool
> God's lesser breed of men at Liverpool.

MICHAEL FOOT in 'Ode to Everton', **1935**.

The delights of the Game are mainly these;
The naked skin to the icy breeze;
The sting of the rain; the nip of the snow;
The whip of the wind, that strikes like a blow;
A charge in the mud; a rueful grin;
Mud on the face; a kick on the shin.
And – though the limbs are afreeze,
The blood's afire within.

G. J. BALLANTINE on 'Schoolboy Soccer' in *The Boy's Own Annual*, **1938–39**.

Red-headed footballer
Four-foot tall
Chalking your goal
on the back-yard wall.

Put boot to the leather,
Go on, shoot!
Let brick, board and hoarding
Feel the force of your boot.

Gas lamp and gable
And chimney-stack –
You'll bring the whole caboodle
Down on your back:

And repenting the ruin
Never at all.
Go whimpering through heaven
For a burst ball.

NORMAN NICHOLSON.

Shote! here's the poliss
The Gayfield poliss,
    and thull pi'iz in the nick fir
    pleyan fi'baw in the street!

ROBERT GARIOCH in 'Fi'baw in the Street'.

The clean programmes are trampled underfoot,
and natural the dark, appropriate the rain,
whilst, under lamposts, threatening newsboys shout.

DANNIE ABSE in 'The Game', **1962**.

HEADMASTER: I see as usual our effort was spoilt by the vociferous minority. The gang who only feel something when they have a red and white scarf round their necks. The people who are only brave in a 50,000 crowd. The people who have got nothing out of school life, and put nothing in. The people who think all the world's a football pitch. For the rest of us, there are more things in life than football.

PETER TERSON in the play *Zigger Zagger*, **1967**, Hymns in school assembly had been disrupted by chants of 'City!'

And that, boys, is how to take a penalty. Look one way, and kick to the other.

SUGDEN, the games teacher (played by Brian Glover) in **1969** film *Kes*, scripted by Barry Hines.

The old architecture of soccer, the grim shabbiness of the corrugated iron age, had gone now. Where once there had been one upright stand and three sides of uncovered, weed-threatened terraces, there were now massive cantilever stands on three sides of the arena, their apparently unsupported roofs jutting dramatically into the blue sky like the dark dorsal fins of monstrous sharks.

GORDON WILLIAMS & TERRY VENABLES in their futuristic novel, *They Used to Play on Grass*, **1971**.

Today even the grass had gone. Commoners had been one of the last clubs in the First Division to install the new plastic turf. In the summer they had dug up the old grass pitch and replaced it with new man made wonder stuff, bright green and totally dead. They had sold off the old pitch at twenty shillings a square foot. People had formed queues to buy a slice of sentimental sod.

WILLIAMS & VENABLES, in *They Used to Play on Grass*, **1971**.

HARRY: Players?. . .Couldn't hold a bloody candle. . . .In them days they'd do a sixteen-hour shift, *then* come up and lake. . . . Nowadays, it's all machines. . .and they're *still* puffed when they come up o' Sat'days. Run round yon field a couple of times: finished. I've seen 'em laking before with broken arms, legs broke. . .shoulders. . . . Get a scratch today, and they're in here, flat on their bloody backs: iodine, liniment, injections. . . . If they ever played a real team today they wouldn't last fifteen bloody seconds. That's my view. That's what I think of them today, Everywhere. There's not one of them that could hold a candle to the past.

DAVID STOREY in *The Changing Room*, a play set in a Rugby League club, **1972**.

I'm a schizofanatic, sad burrits true
One half of me's red, and the other half's blue.
I can't make up me mind which team to support
Whether to lean to starboard or port
I'd be bisexual if I had time for sex
Cos its Goodison one week and Anfield the next.

ROGER McGOUGH, in 'Footy Poem', **1975**.

GRAYSON: Make no mistake, comma, the four-goal credit which these slick Slovaks netted here this afternoon will keep them in the black through the second leg of the World Cup eliminator at Wembley next month, stop. New par.

CHAMBERLAIN: Wilson, who would like to be thought the big bad man of the England defence, merely looked slow-footed and slow-witted, stop. Deml – D.E.M. mother L. – Deml got round him five times on the trot, bracket, literally, close bracket, using the same swerve, comma, making Wilson look elephantine in everything but memory, stop.

TOM STOPPARD in the televison play *Professional Foul*, **1977**. The two reporters are filing copy from a hotel in Prague.

But the pressmen's questions are all the same
'Where's your poem for the derby game?'
I tell them 'Poems don't grow on trees,
    And you ain't forthcoming with any fees!!'

JOHN TOSHACK in *Gosh It's Tosh*, **1976**.

OZ: You know I was saying in the bar the other night about older women, experience and all that beef. Well this one makes Simony Sig-norett look like Shirley Temple. . .When footballers get to a certain age, they've got to slow their game down. . .but they seem to be better players because of experience – like Johnny Giles, Leeds and Eire – I feel like I've been playing with him for 90 minutes this afternoon.

MOXY: Funny you should mention that about footballers, Oz, cos the only older woman I ever had looked like Billy Bremner.

AUF WIEDERSEHEN, PET script by Stan Hey, **1986**.

He's football crazy
He's football mad
And the football it has robbed him
O' the wee bit sense he had.

ROBIN HALL & JIMMY MacGREGOR record, 'Football Crazy', **1960**.

All I want for Christmas is a Dukla Prague away strip.

HALF MAN HALF BISCUIT record title on joys of Subbuteo, **1986**.

O-li O-la
O-li O-la
We're gonna bring that
World Cup home from over tha'.

ROD STEWART song for Scotland's World Cup campaign, **1978**.

We're representing Britain
We've got to do or die
England cannae do it
Cos they didnae qualify.

ANDY CAMERON record 'Ally's Tartan Army', **1978**.

Ossie's going to Wembley, his knees have gone all trembly.

SPURS' FA Cup final record, **1981**.

13
The Oval Codes

American Football

'No, no,' said Pnin, 'do not wish an egg, or, for example, a torpedo. I want a simple football. Round!'

VLADIMIR NABOKOV in the novel *Pnin*, **1957**.

Mon Dieu! This game is war! It has everything.

MARSHALL FOCH at the US Army *v.* Navy game, **1919**.

For when the One Great Scorer comes
To write against your name
He marks – not that you won or lost –
But how you played the game.

GRANTLAND RICE in *Alumnus Football*, *USA*, **1920**.

Someday, Rock, sometime – when the going isn't so easy, when the odds are against us – ask a Notre Dame team to win a game for me, for the Gipper. I don't know where I'll be then, Rock, but I'll know about it and I'll be happy.

DYING WORDS of Notre Dame footballer George Gipp as recorded by his coach, Knute Rockne. Gipp died of pneumonia in **1920**.

Grant, I've never asked the boys to pull one out for Gipp.
Tomorrow I might have to.

KNUTE ROCKNE to sportswriter Grantland Rice before the Army *v.* Notre Dame
match, **1928**.

Here's one of them, Gipper.

JACK CHEVIGNY on scoring a touchdown for Notre Dame *v.* Army, **1928**.

Win it for the Gipper!

POPULAR SAYING.

Outlined against a blue-gray October sky, the Four Horsemen
rode again. In dramatic lore they are known as Famine, Pesti-
lence, Destruction and Death. These are only aliases. Their real
names are Stuhldreher, Miller, Crowley and Layden.

GRANTLAND RICE on the Notre Dame backfield *v.* Army in *New York Herald
Tribune*, **1924**.

At what angle did Rice watch the game to see the Notre Dame
backfield outlined against the sky?

RED SMITH, US sportswriter, *c.* **1960**.

Wild rams butt heads harder than any other animal.

HOMER MARSHMAN, owner of Cleveland Rams (later the LA Rams) on why he
chose the name, **1937**.

Ty-ing is like kissing your sister.

AMERICAN COACH's motto.

When the going gets tough, the tough get going.

AMERICAN COACH's motto.

In football, the Commies are on one side of this ball and we're on the other. That's what this game is all about, make no mistake about it.

JIM RINGO, Green Bay Packers centre, **1959**.

The Mitchell-Agnew-Nixon mentality is what the game is all about. Politics and pro football are the most grotesque extremes in the theatric of a dying empire. It's no accident that the most repressive regime in the history of this country is ruled by a football freak.

DAVE MEGGYESY, pro linebacker with St Louis Cardinals, **1969**.

Hitler was temperamental and had to have his way. He was like some of these football coaches.

LES BANOS, Pittsburgh Steelers official photographer, former Hungarian secret agent and chauffeur to Adolf Eichmann, in Roy Blount Jr, *About Three Bricks Shy of a Load*, **1973**.

Do you want to be the first Notre Dame team to someday tell your grandchildren that you quit?

KNUTE ROCKNE, Notre Dame coach, **1925**.

Men, you've got thirty minutes to play and a lifetime to think about what happened.

DUTCH MEYER, Texas Christian coach, half-time talk, **1933**.

Winning isn't everything – it's the only thing.

VINCE LOMBARDI, Green Bay Packers coach, **1968**.

These aren't truckdrivers – they're artists. Do you understand? Artists!

LOMBARDI to National Football League club owner who referred to players as 'hired hands'.

Win a team's heart and they'll follow you anywhere, do the impossible for you.

LOMBARDI.

The greatest of all achievements is not in never falling, but in rising again after falling.

LOMBARDI.

Lombardi's very fair. He treats us all like dogs.

HENRY JORDAN, Green Bay Packers defensive tackler.

We knew that Lombardi bled inside for us, that he loved us.

BART STARR, Green Bay Packers quarterback.

If the team had lost, I couldn't talk to him. By Thursday, he would say 'hello'. By Friday he would be almost human. On Saturday he was civil. By Sunday he might even smile a little.

MARIE LOMBARDI, wife of Vince, **1981**. Lombardi died of cancer in 1970.

People thought he was fierce and ruthless. In truth, he was just a kitten. At home, Vince could be a tyrant one minute and a pussycat the next. He kept everything on edge. You never knew when the next explosion would occur.

MARIE LOMBARDI, **1981**.

A good coach needs a patient wife, a loyal dog and a great quarterback, but not necessarily in that order.

BUD GRANT, Minnesota Vikings coach, **1970**.

It's an immense game all right, but keep it in proportion – there are 600 million Chinese who don't give a damn whether we win or lose.

JOHNNY McKAY, University of Southern California (USC) coach, to his squad before game *v*. Notre Dame, **1973**.

Pressure is what you feel when you don't know how to do your job.

CHUCK NOLL, Pittsburgh Steelers coach, in Roy Blount Jr, *About Three Bricks Shy of a Load*, **1973**.

Two kinds of football players ain't worth a damn. One that never does what he's told and the other who does nothing except what he's told.

BUM PHILLIPS, New Orleans Saints coach, **1984**.

I left the job for reasons of ill-health and fatigue. The fans were sick and tired of me.

KANSAS CHIEFS coach, early **1970s**.

There's nothing football coaches love more than to watch two guys really pounding the shit out of each other.

DAVE MEGGYESY, St Louis Cardinals outside linebacker, in *Out of Their League*, **1971**.

All coaches consider themselves great amateur psycholoigsts, and feel they can read a player's soul in his face. This accounts for a common saying among players: 'Here comes the coach, put on your game face.'

DAVE MEGGYESY.

When we're losing, I like to see a guy really crumple some people.

BRUCE VAN DYKE, Pittsburgh Steelers offensive guard, in Roy Blount Jr, *About Three Bricks Shy of A Load*, **1973**.

Don't be a 'nice guy' and just tackle the receiver, make him remember you and never want to catch another ball in your area again.

PITTSBURGH STEELERS playbook, **1972**.

You get in a good lick around the head area, it rattles the man. You can beat a dazed man easier than an alert one. It's that simple.

CHRIS HAMBURGER, Washington Redskins player.

If I can hit a man hard enough so he has to be carried off the field, I'll be glad to help him off.

DEACON JONES, LA Rams player, **1969**.

My idea of a good hit is when the victim wakes up on the sidelines with train whistles blowing in his head. I like to believe that my best hits border on felonious assault.

JACK TATUM, Oakland Raiders free safety, in *They Call Me Assassin*, **1979**.

Throwing a football is comparable to painting a canvas or playing a piano. You have to practise often enough to stay at a high performance level. The difference is that Beethoven didn't play the 'Moonlight Sonata' and van Gogh didn't paint the 'Potato Eaters' with Mean Joe Greene charging at them from the blind side.

JIM PLUNKETT, Oakland Raiders quarterback, in *The Jim Plunkett Story*, **1981**.

I wasn't only to be a professional football player talking about my craft, but – especially when youngsters were present – I was supposed to give an inspiring talk about sports, patriotism and mental hygiene. I had the spiel down pretty well. I had never been taught it, but it is next to impossible to play football without it becoming part of you.

DAVE MEGGYESY, in *Out of Their League*, **1971**.

I see my job as a part of American civilization and as a damn
important part. I see football as being just so much above everything else. Now when you think about what's happened in this
country in the last few goddamned years you begin to wonder just
how much longer we're going to last. We used to take the team
out to a good movie the Friday night before a game, but this is a
real sonofabitch of a problem now. We were playing up in Minnesota and we took the boys to see *Easy Rider* and it really shook
'em up. We won it, but it was a squeaker. Now I have to get my
coaches scout the movies we see so these kids don't get hurt.

WOODY HAYES, Ohio State University coach, in Robert Vare, *Buckeye*, 1974.

College football is a great spectacle, but I am not sure that it gives
an accurate picture of America. To see some of our best-educated
boys spending an afternoon knocking each other down – while
thousands cheer them on – hardly gives a picture of a peace-loving
nation.

PRESIDENT JOHNSON advising against taking a visiting Laotian Prince and Princess
to watch Stanford, 1967.

Personally, I am glad that thousands of fine Americans can spend
this Saturday afternoon 'knocking each other down' in a spirit of
clean sportsmanship and keen competition instead of assaulting
Pentagon soldiers or policemen with 'peace' placards and filthy
words.

GERALD FORD, then House minority leader, replying to LBJ.

I've always said that in life, as well as in sports, politics and
business, what really makes a team of a country is when it has
lost one, it doesn't lose its spirit. I think this team has the spirit
it takes. I think this government has it. You're going to go on
and win.

PRESIDENT NIXON to the Washington Redskins, 1971.

He's really hurting us. He calls us all the time. I think I'm going to ask George Allen to tell the President not to talk about the game until after we've played it.

BILLY KILMER, Washington Redskins quarterback, after losing to San Francisco. Defeat was ascribed to a play sent down to coach Allen by Nixon.

It troubles me that he played center. He can only consider options for twenty yards in either direction and. . .He has spent a good deal of his life looking at the world upside down through his legs.

MARTIN PERETZ, editorial director *New Republic*, on the arrival of Gerald Ford as President, **1974**.

Ford played too many games without wearing a helmet.

PRESIDENT JOHNSON, several years earlier.

I can't understand how the President [Nixon] can know so little about Watergate in 1973 and so much about college football in 1969.

JOE PATERNO, Penn State University coach, **1974**.

I like it [the national anthem] played. Every time I hear it before a game, it reminds me of where we are in the world, in life. I kind of thank God we're in this country. When I hear it I get a chill.

JOE NAMATH, New York Jets quarterback, four months before Nixon put him on the White House 'enemies' list, **1973**.

I don't know, man, I've never smoked Astroturf.

NAMATH, when asked whether he preferred Astroturf to grass.

SportsWorld's 'mod' or 'swinging' faction made excuses for Namath's lifestyle – it was 'today'. Actually, Namath's lifestyle was yesterday, a kind of Drugstore Cowboy Cool clothed as Sixties Singlestud Chic.

ROBERT LIPSYTE, writer, in *Sportsworld: an American Dreamland*, **1977**.

Ball players, like beer salesmen and advertising executives, talk continually about sex, about the need to get laid and how they themselves almost got laid quite recently. The way they talk, players seem to see sex as something close to athletics. They worry a lot about 'staying power' and 'performance' and dream of being able to inspire a string of orgasms in a woman the same way they dream of single-handedly making a long series of tackles.

DAVE MEGGYESY, in *Out of Their League*, **1971**.

They let you chase girls, they just don't let you catch them.

GLEN KOZLOWSKI, Brigham Young University captain, on the Mormon church's influence on his team, **1985**.

A great negotiator makes much more money than a great running back.

PETER GENT, ex-Dallas Cowboys player, in novel *North Dallas Forty*, **1973**.

The thing that makes cocaine what it is today in the NFL, is that for football players it duplicates the incredible emotional high they can get on the field. Now a player can get the same thrill from cocaine that he got running ninety yards for a touchdown. And they don't actually have to do it any more. They can get the same feeling from the end of a pipe, and all you have to do is to have the money for it.

CARL ELLER, Minnesota Vikings defensive lineman, **1983**.

Kids in my part of Texas would rather play football than eat.

Y. A. (YELVERTON ABRAHAM) TITTLE, New York Giants quarterback, **1963**.

I'm a light eater. As soon as it's light, I start to eat.

ART DONOVAN, former 310-1b defensive lineman with the Baltimore Colts, **1980**.

This football business is like a day off compared to what I did on the farm as a youngster. You don't get patted on the back or written up in the press for picking cotton.

LEE ROY JORDAN, Dallas Cowboys player, **1970**.

Nothing recedes like success. The journey from penthouse to outhouse can be a quick one.

JIM PLUNKETT, Oakland Raiders quarterback, **1980**.

They said I looked like Tarzan and played like Jane.

DENNIS HARRISON, 6ft 8in, 275–lb footballer on why he had been passed over by the NFL clubs.

I feel like Job. I'd rather be the Phoenix rising from the ashes, but the ashes just keep piling up.

BERL BERNHARD, owner of Washington Federals, 'losingest' team in USFL, the summer league founded in **1983**.

My Super Bowl ring may end up in the gutter, but if it does, I'll be wearing it.

MARK MOSELEY, Washington Redskins placekicker, **1983**.

I'm sure the British public will wonder why the players have so much protective equipment. What they'll be watching is disciplined violence. At ground level you can hear the impact. When two 250-lb players run into each other, it's like ammunition.

PETER ROZELLE, NFL Commissioner, at Wembley for Minnesota v. St. Louis, **1983**.

I'd like to apologize to the man who won the name-the-team contest and got a ticket for life.

PAUL MARTHA, Pittsburgh Maulers' president, on the club's demise after one season, **1985**.

It was so muddy, people planted rice at half-time.

TONY MEO, college coach in Pennsylvania, **1985**.

We don't have any Refrigerators. We do have a few pot-belly stoves, but they're on the coaching staff.

DAVE CURREY, University of Cincinatti coach, on the William Perry phenomenon, **1986**.

I wouldn't want to play rugby. That's a very dangerous game.

ST LOUIS CARDINALS PLAYER at Wembley, **1983**.

When your defense gives up more points than your basketball team, you've got big trouble.

LOU HOLTZ, Minnesota University coach, **1984**.

I've already gotten a call from Moscow. They think Marcus Allen [LA Raiders' running back] is a new secret weapon. They insist we dismantle it.

PRESIDENT RONALD REAGAN after **1984** Super Bowl.

Football is an attempt to sell a blown-out, smacked-out people, fighting inflation, the exploitation of their work, of their earth, of Vietnamese and American Indians, that our system is still socially, economically and politically viable. Pro football keeps telling them you can't be second-rate, you have to be winners.

DAVE MEGGYESY, St. Louis Cardinals, **1969**.

Without winners there wouldn't even be any goddamned civilization.

WOODY HAYES, Ohio State University coach, in Robert Vare, *Buckeye*, **1974**.

Don't you just loathe American Football? What kind of game is it where they spend 5% of the time actually playing, and the other 95% planning it out, or celebrating it? Violence, macho posing, drugs, money, yeah, yeah, yeah! All this interest in it is really disturbing – it says a lot about Britain's slide into trashy American decadence. Burger culture. The thing that really condemns American society is their total failure to come to terms with soccer. It's the clearest indication possible of a sick society.

WHEN SATURDAY COMES, British soccer fanzine, **1986**.

This isn't a contact sport – it's a collision sport.

MIKE DITKA, Chicago Bears coach, **1986**.

Australian Rules

Without wishing to give offence to anyone, I may remark that it is a game which commends itself to semi-barbarous races. . . .It is even contended, that the fact that it raises such enthusiasm, even to the point of broken heads and bloody noses, is a conclusive argument that it is the best of all games.

EDWARD KINGLAKE, author, *The Australian at Home*, **1891**.

It might best be described as a game devised for padded cells, played in the open air.

JAMES MURRAY, journalist, in *Walkabout* magazine (Melbourne), **1967**.

Rugby League

The Man's Game For All The Family.

RUGBY LEAGUE marketing slogan, **1981**.

The Northern Union [Rugby League] is sometimes referred to as a moribund organization, and there are those who express the belief that its extinction is only a matter of a few more seasons. Probably this is, in some instances, a case of pious wish rather than an expression of honest conviction.

J. H. SMITH, Northern Union president, in the *Book of Football*, **1906**. The break with amateur Rugby Union had come in 1895.

Where I was born, babes don't toddle, they sidestep: queuing women talk of 'nipping round the blindside'; Rugby League provides a cultural adrenalin, a physical manifestation of our rules of life, comradeship, honest endeavour and a staunch, often ponderous allegiance to fair play.

COLIN WELLAND, Warrington-born playwright-actor and Fulham RL director, **1980**.

One of the great myths about Rugby League is that it is a job, not a game, and that we are grim-faced professionals in it only for the money.

TOMMY DAVID, Cardiff City prop and ex-Rugby Union international, **1984**.

Sometimes I feel overpaid and underworked when I go to Rugby League.

BOBBY CHARLTON on visit to Salford, **1969**.

I don't care what colour jersey I wear as long as the pound notes are green.

RUGBY LEAGUE INTERNATIONAL PLAYER on his transfer request, **1981**.

Against Workington a big forward came bundling through the middle and was confronted with me. He pushed me off and I landed on my backside in the mud. The crowd on the popular side groaned. It happened a second and a third time. The fourth time it happened, one exasperated wag shouted, 'For Christ's sake Watkins, hit him with your wallet.'

DAVID WATKINS on his lucrative switch from Newport RU to Salford RL in **1967**.

When he first came to Salford everybody had a go at him. I hit him, everybody in our team hit him, in fact almost everyone in the League hit him. But he just got up and kept playing. Great player.

REGGIE BOWDEN, then Widnes scrum-half, on David Watkins's switch, **1979**.

If I tried to count up to ten, I probably wouldn't make three. The old blue mist comes rolling in front of my eyes and that's it. He goes down and I go off.

JIM MILLS, Widnes forward, on being sent off twenty times, **1978**.

When Jim Mills tackles someone he almost squeezes them to death, he's got such bloody big arms. He's a great deterrent too. When Jim stands in the middle of the park, nobody fights our team. Not if they've got any sense, they don't. But you get lunatics, mainly big young lads, who think they can make their name by taking Jim on. There was a Wigan feller who had a go at him in the first half. He didn't wake up until half-an-hour after the match. But he never hits anyone first.

REGGIE BOWDEN, Widnes captain, **1979**.

I'm as thick as pigshit, I'm slow and I'm a coward. If a really hard man like, say, Jim Mills hit me, I'd just say 'Go on, do it again if it makes you happy.'

STEVE NORTON, Hull forward, **1982**.

People say black sportsmen can't take the knocks. But there have been coloured players in Rugby League for a long time now. Frank Wilson, Colin Dixon and my boyhood hero Billy Boston for instance – and this is a very physical game.

CLIVE SULLIVAN, Hull Kingston Rovers and Great Britain winger, **1980**.

The sort of tackle that got him [Paul Ringer] sent off at Twickenham happens in every Rugby League match. He's a big, tough lad but no more vicious than a lot of players in our game.

JIM MILLS, ex-Widnes and Great Britain prop, **1981**.

Tennis players are a load of wankers. I'd love to put McEnroe in the centre for Fulham and let some of those big rugby players sort him out.

COLIN WELLAND, Fulham director, **1981**.

My wife doesn't want me to walk through the town and have people pointing and saying, 'That's him. He's *sine die*. Dirty Dalgreen.' I'm not really dirty. I'm very kind and generous. I'm very quiet off the field, a family man. I don't drink very much and I don't smoke. I like to potter around the home. I'm not a ruffian. I'm really not.

JOHN DALGREEN, Fulham hooker, on his life ban, **1983**.

I wouldn't play the French at marbles, never mind Rugby League. All we'll ever learn off them is how to fight and spit and bite each other.

ALEX MURPHY, Wigan coach, **1984**.

These great Australians are one of the greatest rugby teams ever to visit our shores. They would rank with the 1951 Springboks, 1967 All Blacks and 1971 Lions in New Zealand. Their professionalism is such that, with two extra men, they would convincingly beat any of the four home countries at the Rugby Union game.

CLEM THOMAS, ex-British Lions RU player, on **1982** Australian RL tourists.

The Australians have shown us up for what we are – no bloody good.

REGGIE BOWDEN, Fulham player-coach, **1982**.

These Australians are from another planet.

ALEX MURPHY, Wigan coach, on **1982** tourists.

They pay good money in Australia but they also want their pound of flesh. Some players will do practically anything to get out on the field. My club, Penrith, never gave me drugs – I bought them without Penrith knowing. I've seen a fair number of opponents packing down against me with glazed eyes that certainly didn't come from wintergreen or rubbing oil.

MICK STEPHENSON, former Great Britain and Dewsbury hooker, on his time with the Australian club Penrith, **1978**.

I still think Huyton can make something of it. There's potential here, the lot, club and ground and players. The money's the bugger.

GEOFF FLETCHER, veteran player-coach, on the game's worst-supported club, **1982**.

We're not in it for the honour, we're in it for the brass.

ERNIE CLAY, Fulham soccer chairman, on applying for RL membership, **1980**.

The Carlisle board seemed to view the Rugby League club like a publican might view a jukebox. Install it. Watch it twinkle. Enjoy the music, but take it out the moment it shows signs of losing money.

DAVID HOWES, League PRO, on the near-collapse of one of the 'expansionist' clubs, **1983**.

I want to sell Rugby League to the local people. The match ball for our first game will be brought to the pitch by parachute. We also plan to have majorettes and Morris dancers. After all, this is Kent.

PAUL FAIRES, Kent Invicta's first chairman, **1983**.

Just as London decrees that screen Scotsmen must wear kilts and eat haggis, with Welshmen shouting 'look you' every few moments, so it sees Rugby League as a game for ape-like creatures watched by gloomy men in cloth caps. To London 'the North' is one long Coronation Street where everyone devours daily helpings of Yorkshire pudding and Lancashire hot-pot. The League grounds are rather seedy arenas where twenty-six gladiators knock each other around in order to earn enough for a bag of chips and a pint of dark ale after the match.

DAVID WATKINS, former Salford RL and Wales RU captain, in *An Autobiography*, **1980**.

Eddie Waring has done for our game what Cyril Smith has done for hang-gliding.

REGGIE BOWDEN, Fulham player-coach, **1980**.

If that's a local derby, it's a good job we don't play Rotherham.

TOM MORTON, Doncaster's general manager, after five players had been sent off in first 20 minutes *v*. Sheffield Eagles, **1986**.

In the eyes of Rugby Union, having a game of Rugby League – either amateur or professional – is like introducing Aids to the dressing-room.

ALEX MURPHY, St Helens coach, **1986**.

I was ugly enough through Rugby Union. I'd hate to think what I'd look like if I had ten years with the League. It's that much harder. And that much faster.

TOMMY DAVID, Cardiff City prop, **1984**.

On Mondays, which I set aside for developing skills and positional play, there were sometimes only four or five players turning up. From the others I'd get excuses like 'My wife was having a tupper-ware party'.

GEOFF WRAITH on his resignation as Wakefield Trinity coach, **1984**.

I am not a scientist and I am not talking to brain surgeons.

GRAHAM LOWE, New Zealand coach, **1985**.

It's not Terry Holmes that Bradford need – it's Sherlock.

ALEX MURPHY, **1985**.

The main difference between League and Union is that now I get my hangovers on Mondays instead of Sundays.

TOMMY DAVID, ex-British Lions RU forward, **1983**.

Rugby Union

Rugby must always be amateur, which means playing in one's spare time for recreation. If a man wants to play professional rugby, good luck to him. But there is no room for him in our game.

w. w. (LORD) WAKEFIELD, former England captain and RFU president, in Cliff Morgan, *Rugby: The Great Ones*, **1970**.

It has already fallen to the lot of famous Rugby players to figure conspicuously in the feats and sacrifices of the war. In the recent naval action Lieutenant Arthur Harrison was in charge of two 13.5 guns and must have had the privilege of firing some of the first shots.

THE FIELD, 30 January **1915**.

Every town must have its sewer.

JAMES BAXTER, British Lions tour manager, when asked why he thought Rugby League was so popular in Auckland, **1930**.

He was grimy; his scrum cap was torn; and his jersey was split. His best friend wouldn't have recognized him. Then his scrum cap was torn off his head and I heard a shrill childish voice cry, 'Look! Look! There's Daddy!' A thousand or more eyes turned and saw a little girl of about three sitting by her young mother. And the player, who was the terror of his opponents, looked up, his mouth parted with a loving smile. He waved his hand for one fleeting moment, and then he dived at a man who had the ball under his arm. 'Wakefield again!' ejaculated a man at my side. 'Isn't he wonderful?'

F. B. DOUGLAS-HAMILTON on W. W. Wakefield, England captain, in *The Boy's Own Annual*, **1933–34**.

You can't play first-class Rugger if you are dressed third-class, any more than you can sit on a public vehicle while a lady is standing, and remain a gentleman.

AN OLD BEDFORD BOY on 'Some Rudiments Of Rugger' in *The Boy's Own Annual*, **1933–34**.

To become (a Compleat Footballer) your budding centre should live with a rugby ball just as your would-be bowler should always have a cricket ball in his pocket, except of course in church.

E. H. D. SEWELL, Bedford School and Harlequins, in *The Boy's Own Annual*, **1934–35**.

When you stride on to the pitch to do or die for your school, don't leave your brains in the dressing-room. They are very useful 'out in the middle'. For Rugger, properly played, *is a brainy game*, even though brawn is not a negligible concomitant.

E. H. D. SEWELL, *The Boy's Own Annual*, **1934–35**.

It is a form of *cowardice*, nothing else, this overdoing of the punt by backs in whichever direction they are facing.

E. H. D. SEWELL, *The Boy's Own Annual*, **1934–35**.

> Old Rugger – shorts and jersey,
> A field, twin goals – a ball;
> What reck we of the weather
> A hack, a charge, a fall?
> There's joy for youthful Britons,
> When Rugger comes again!

HAROLD DORNING in 'When Rugger Comes Again?' in *Boy's Own Paper*, **1939**.

You have to respect the opposition. Even if you win by 100 points it's not their fault they're on the field. I still want to have a drink with them afterwards.

BARRY JOHN, Wales back, **1971**.

Get your retaliation in first.

CARWYN JAMES, British Lions coach, **1971**.

I prefer rugby to soccer. . . . I enjoy the violence in rugby, except when they start biting each other's ears off.

ELIZABETH TAYLOR, film star, **1972**.

Welsh supporters are one-eyed and Welsh players are cheats.

SID GOING, New Zealand scrum-half, **1974**.

Look what these b— have done to Wales. They've taken our coal, our water, our steel, they buy our houses and they only live in them a fortnight every twelve months. What have they given us. . .absolutely nothing. We've been exploited, raped, controlled and punished by the English – and that's who you are playing this afternoon.

PHIL BENNETT, Wales captain, before match against England, **1977**.

Never mind, you had the nicest jerseys.

WELSH SUPPORTER to chairman of England selectors after Wales's 27–3 win, **1979**.

I discovered the difference between English and Welsh rugby during my National Service. Playing at fly-half for the Navy I was surprised when I worked the touchline to hear the cultured English tones of the pack-leader thanking me most graciously for my sterling efforts. At home, at Llanelli, you only heard the pack-leader when you missed a touch kick. You did not miss a second time.

CARWYN JAMES, former British Lions coach, **1980**.

It was like MASH in the medical room.

LEON WALKDEN, RFU doctor, after violent England v. Wales match, **1980**.

I thought we'd gone to Twickenham when the game started. I thought the Welsh Rugby Union team had taken over.

BOB PAISLEY, Liverpool FC manager, after bitter Merseyside derby, **1980**.

I will not allow my son to play. Besides, he has told me himself he would rather give up rugby than scrum down with them [blacks].

F. J. MEINTJIES, leading South African Nationalist Party member, on 'relaxation' of apartheid laws, **1980**.

Colin [Smart] may not have looked too good, but I'm told he smelled lovely.

STEVE SMITH, England captain, after the prop had allegedly collapsed after drinking aftershave at Paris banquet, **1982**.

It was about par for a rugby dinner. . .from what I can remember.

COLIN SMART.

The aftershave'll flow tonight.

STEVE SMITH after victory over Wales a month later.

I don't like threats. We've been threatened by Germans before in this country, but they've always been knocked down.

ARTHUR YOUNG, 'mole' in the Adidas 'boot money' affair, **1982**.

Rugby is different in Wales and there are far more working-class lads playing than in England. The odd £50 makes a lot of difference.

ARTHUR YOUNG.

On the club circuit in England and Wales, there are roughly a dozen players whom I'd describe as psychopathic thugs. I don't think that's going over the top. In the context of what happened to me, that description is not too strong.

JOHN DAVIDSON, Moseley prop, forced to retire after his jaw and cheekbone were fractured by a Swansea player, **1983**.

There's so much playing a man off the ball here [in New Zealand] that one day someone might get killed.

WILLIE JOHN MCBRIDE, British Lions' tour manager, **1983**.

Rugby can be a very violent game if there is £1000 a man riding on the result.

BOB WEIGHILL, RFU secretary, on the proposed professional 'circus', **1983**.

If you are 6ft 7in and can jump in the line-out, you can play international Rugby Union.

BOB MORDELL, ex-England RU forward, and an RL player, later, **1984**.

The knee injury does not trouble me when I'm walking. But it's painful when I kneel, like before the bank manager.

DAVID LESLIE, Scottish international, **1984**.

Like you (we) came under the yoke of our Anglo-Saxon brothers. You, wisely, though, had much more sense than us, in that you devoured as many as you could.

ALAN THOMAS, Welsh RU president, welcoming the Fijian tourists, **1985**.

To stamp out dirty play we need leadership and authority. When I was a referee I never sent off anyone in 13 years. If there was any spiky business I would immediately show the players who was boss.

DENIS THATCHER, the Prime Minister's husband, **1985**.

I told them, 'Fellows, I am not prepared to condone this type of street violence'. . .Before going, I told the players, 'You obviously don't need me.'

GEORGE CRAWFORD, referee who walked off after 20 minutes of violent Bristol *v.* Newport match, **1985**.

I've even been made Capital Radio's man of the week. I believe I get seven Sacha Distel records. It's the only thing that's made me wonder whether I made the right decision.

GEORGE CRAWFORD.

We hope we'll be playing each other again on a regular basis. Time is a great healer. After all, we trade with Japan.

ALAN SKEATS, Richmond president, on resumption of fixtures with Llanelli six years after falling out over rough play, **1985**.

I played 10 injury-free years between the ages of 12 and 22. Then suddenly it seemed I was allergic to the twentieth century.

NIGEL MELVILLE, England captain on his succession of injuries, **1984**.

If Wales went to war with Russia tomorrow, I honestly reckon the Welsh would stand a bloody good chance.

ANDREW SLACK, Australia's captain, before game v. Wales, **1984**.

No leadership, no ideas. Not even enough imagination to thump someone in the line-out when the ref wasn't watching.

J. P. R. WILLIAMS after Wales's defeat by Australians, **1984**.

It didn't demoralise us, but it moralised them.

DICK GREENWOOD, England coach, on handling error that cost a try in defeat by Wales, **1985**.

I take the Gucci view about hard work on the practice field – long after you have forgotten the price, the quality remains.

ALAN JONES, coach of the Australian tourists, **1984**.

14
Sick as a Paraguayan – World Cup 1986

The Animals Are Coming.

El Sol (Monterrey) headline on the prospect of England fans' visit.

We do not believe there will be trouble. Because of the cost of getting here, we expect an upper middle-class sort of person, the type who represents the British tradition of education. . . ., Like gentlemen, like an officer trained at Sandhurst. Someone like David Niven.

GUILLERMO URQUIGO, Monterrey Police spokesman, on the kind of English visitor he hoped for.

Brazil is all smiles. Officials, coaches, players, sportswriters and fans are certain of our qualifying for the second round. Now all we need is a team.

Jornal do Brasil on the World Cup draw.

It's every player's dream to turn out against Brazil, and to tuck one of their shirts in the drawer.

BILLY HAMILTON, Northern Ireland striker.

It would be much harder if it were the world ice hockey championships.

JOEL BATS, France goalkeeper, on being drawn with Canada and the Soviet Union.

This for me is without exception possibly my last World Cup.

RAY WILKINS, England midfielder, before flying out to Mexico.

In case there is an earthquake, FIFA have set up an emergency committee.

HANS NEUBERGER, FIFA vice-president.

The memory of this day will live in the memory.

JOAO HAVELANGE, FIFA president, at the Opening Ceremony.

Queremos Frijoles No Goles (We want beans not goals).

MEXICAN STEELWORKERS' banner at the opening ceremony.

I couldn't believe the way Platini spoke to his team-mates. He was always yapping and yelling.

RANDY SAMUEL, Canada's centre-half, after defeat by France.

I hope the people will show enough respect to applaud us in the final.

DIEGO MARADONA, 'hurt' by crowd's booing Argentina in their first match v. South Korea.

The Iraqis don't take any prisoners.

RON ATKINSON, ITV.

We had a Mauritian referee against Paraguay. Mauritius is a lovely island, but they don't play football.

EVARISTO MACEDA, Iraqi coach.

Anyone who knows the Irish knows that when we're provoked we sometimes bite.

BILLY BINGHAM, Northern Ireland manager, after drawing with the 'spitting' Algerians.

I may have a German passport, but I have a Danish heart.

SEPP PIONTEK, German-born manager of Denmark.

It's like you're going to war. If you lose, people want to see you shot.

OMAR BORRAS, Uruguayan manager, on death threats received after Denmark 6, Uruguay 1.

There was a murderer on the pitch – the referee.

OMAR BORRAS on the Italian official who sent off one of his Uruguayan defenders after 40 seconds *v*. Scotland.

I'm glad we're going home. For Borras to defend his team, to sit there lying and cheating, is farcical.

ALEX FERGUSON, Scotland manager, after the ugly 0–0 draw with Uruguay.

I will change my name to Jose Mehedi (the Great God) when I return to Rabat.

JOSE FARIA, Morocco's Brazilian-born manager.

Beckenbauer is like Humpty Dumpty, and the team are playing like a bunch of cucumbers.

ULLI STEIN, West Germany's No 3 goalkeeper, sent home for criticising his colleagues.

Fingers crossed for more glorious goals from gorgeous Gary. And if all goes well, we'll stuff the Argies on Sunday.

Sun editorial before England *v*. Paraguay. After England's win the paper gloated 'Now we know what it means to be sick as a Paraguayan'.

The Pope may be Polish, but God is a Brazilian.

PELE, after Brazil 4, Poland 0 in second phase.

I'll wager my watch on Italy. It's a gold Cartier. They will leave France by the wayside.

DIEGO MARADONA on the second phase match. . .France 2, Italy 0.

The Bluff Finishes.

Corriere della Sport headline after Italy's exit.

Two Gary Stevens, there's only two Gary Stevens. . .

ENGLAND FANS' song in Mexico City.

Conjugate the verb 'done great': I done great. He done great. We done great. They done great. The boy Lineker done great.

LETTER to *The Guardian*.

I wouldn't blame anyone for not turning up. I'm sure the Almighty will understand.

REV. DICK ACWORTH of St Mary's Church, Taunton, on fears of a low attendance on the evening of Argentina *v*. England.

Maradona can win a game on his own in five minutes.

BOBBY ROBSON before the quarter-finals. Maradona took him at his word.

A little bit the hand of God, a little the head of Diego.

DIEGO MARADONA on his 'volleyball' goal against England.

We blasted the English pirates with Maradona and a little hand. He who robs a thief has a thousand years of pardon.

CRONICA newspaper of Buenos Aires, under the headline 'Malvinas 2, Inglese 1'.

It didn't seem to worry Maradona, did it?

GARY LINEKER answering colleagues' criticisms of the Azteca Stadium pitch.

I won't be going anywhere near the German goal – no closer than 40 metres.

PATRICK BATTISTON on renewing acquaintance with Harald Schumacher, the goalkeeper whose 'tackle' in Seville four years earlier put him out of the game for a year.

Football is important but life is important too.

MAXIME BOSSIS of France after semi-final defeat.

I went over in my mind my decisions, my selections, my preparations, and everything else that could have contributed to our exit. There was absolutely nothing I would have changed.

BOBBY ROBSON.

This is a poor Argentine team.

CESAR MENOTTI, manager of Argentina's world champions of 1978, before the final.

Maradona, porque no naciste en Mexico? (Why weren't you born in Mexico?)

BANNER at the final.

Leave me alone. I can't speak now.

CARLOS BILARDO, Argentina's manager, in tears after their victory in the final.

If our lot (Liverpool) had been out here, we'd have done the treble.

JAN MOLBY, Denmark midfielder.

With Maradona, even Arsenal would have won it.

BOBBY ROBSON.

Select Bibliography

Sources of material and inspiration:

The All-American War Game, James Lawton, (Basil Blackwell, 1984)

Anatomy of Football Star: George Best, David Meek, (Arthur Barker, 1970)

Association Football and English Society 1863–1915, Tony Mason, (Harvester, 1980)

Association Football and the Men who made it, Alfred Gibson and William Pickford, [1906)

Barnsley – A Study in Football 1953–59, Ian Alister and Andrew Ward, (Crowberry, 1981)

Black and White Magic, Jim Paterson and Douglas Scott, (Dunfermline, 1984).

Blackpool Football, Robin Daniels, (Robert Hale Books, 1972)

Blowing the Whistle: The Politics of Sport, Garry Whannel, (Pluto Press, 1983)

The Boys of '66, Martin Tyler, (Hamlyn, 1981)

Buckeye: Coach Woody Hayes and the Ohio State Football Machine, Robert Vare, (Harper's Magazine Press, USA, 1974)

Clown Prince of Soccer, Len Shackleton, (Nicholas Kaye, 1955)

Corinthians, Casuals and Cricketers, Edward Grayson, (Naldrett Press, 1955)

Don't Shoot the Goalkeeper, Jonathan Croall, (Oxford University Press, 1976)

The Education of an American Soccer Player, Shep Messing, (Dodd, Mead & Co, USA, 1978)

The Encyclopedia of Association Football, Edited by Geoffrey Green et al, (Caxton, 1960)

The European Cup 1955–80, John Motson and John Rowlinson, (Queen Anne Press, 1980)

The Football Man, Arthur Hopcraft, (Collins, 1968)

The Football Managers, Tony Pawson, (Eyre Methuen, 1973)

The Foul Book of Football No. 1, Edited by Andrew Nickolds and Stan Hey, (1976)

The Glory Game, Hunter Davies, (Sphere, 1972)

Great Masters of Scottish Football, Hugh Taylor, (Stanley Paul, 1967)

A History of British Football, Percy M. Young, (Stanley Paul, 1968)

The History of The World Cup, Brian Glanville, (Faber and Faber, 1980)

Journey to Wembley, Brian James, (Marshall Cavendish, 1977)

Kicked into Touch, Fred Eyre, (Senior Publications, 1981)

A Man For All Seasons, Steve Perryman, (Arthur Barker, 1985)

The Manchester United Aircrash, Max Arthur, (Aquarius Books, 1983)

Nice Guys Finish Last, Paul Gardner, (Allen Lane, 1974)

Only a Game?, Eamon Dunphy, (Kestrel, 1976)

One Hundred Years of Scottish Football, John Rafferty, (Pan, 1973)

100 Years of Welsh Soccer, Peter Corrigan, (Welsh Brewers Ltd, 1976)

Out of Their League, Dave Meggyesy, (Ramparts Press Inc, USA, 1971)

Pele: My Life and the Beautiful Game, Pele with Robert L. Fish, (Doubleday & Co. Inc, USA, 1977)

Sir Alf Ramsey: Anatomy of a Football Manager, Max Marquis, (Arthur Barker, 1970)

Soccer Rebel, Jimmy Guthrie, (Readers' Union, 1976)

Soccer: The Road to Crisis, Anton Rippon, (Moorland Publishing Co., 1983)

SportsWorld: An American Dreamland, Robert Lipsyte, (Quadrangle, USA, 1977)

The Team from a Town of Chimneys, Stewart Beckett, (Comprehensive Art Services, 1982)

When Will We See Your like Again?, Edited by Mike Aitken, (EUSPB Edinburgh, 1977)

With Clough By Taylor, Peter Taylor, (Sidgwick and Jackson, 1980)

World Cup: The Argentina Story, David Miller, (Frederick Warne, 1978)

Index

Football is my Passport (Wright), 35, 196
Football Man (Hopcraft), 32, 113, 125, 151, 155, 171, 193, 197
The Football Managers (Pawson), 17, 52, 64, 76, 80, 83, 104, 112
Football with the Millionaires (Firmani), 188, 189
Football as a Profession (Dougan & Young), 174
Football World, 93
Football Worlds (Rous), 115
Football Year (Young), 104, 113, 218
Ford, President Gerald, 237
Forfar Athletic, 92, 147
Fort Lauderdale Strikers, 126
Forward, Arsenal! (Joy), 135
Foster, Steve, 207
Foul! Book of Football (Nickolds and Hey), 48, 104
Foulke, William 'Fatty', 22, 52, 161
France, 152, 254, 255, 257, 258
Francis, Tony, 221
Francis, Trevor, 118, 125
Franklin, Neil, Soccer at Home and Abroad, 21, 108, 110, 152
Frizzell, Jimmy, 128
Fry, C. B., 19, 92, 100
Fulham FC, 114, 160, 176, 178, 181, 190, 200
Fulham RL, 242, 245, 246

Gabriel, Jimmy, 186
Gallacher, Hughie, 23
Garioch, Robert, 227
Garrincha, 117
Gedge, Paul, 130
Gemmill, Archie, 38, 75
Genders, Harold, 246
Gent, Peter, North Dallas Forty, 137, 215, 239
Gentile, Claudio, 125
The Gentle Giant (Charles), 120, 141, 196
Gento, Francisco, 34, 35, 38, 54
Germany, 155
  see also West Germany
Gibson, Alfred, Association Football and the Men Who Made It, 22, 44, 53, 55, 95, 96, 194, 212–13
Gibson, Terry, 164
Gidman, John, 71
Giles, John, 23, 82, 100, 162
Gilzean, George, 231
Gipp, George, 231
Give a Little Whistle (Hill), 185
Glanville, Brian, The History of the World Cup, 39
Glasgow Rangers, 11, 45, 53, 54, 147, 200, 205
Gloria, Otto, 39

The Glory Game (Davies), 65, 101, 105, 146, 147, 189, 197–8
Goalkeeper's Fear of the Penalty, 150
Goering, Hermann, 155
Going, Sid, 250
The Good Companions (Priestley), 226
Goodall, John, 113, 129, 151
Goodbye to Yorkshire (Hattersley), 182, 197
Gould, Bobby, 105
Grant, Bud, 234
Graveney, David, 167
Gray, Andy, 114
Gray, Eddie, 23
Grayson, Edward, Corinthians, Casuals and Cricketers, 45, 129, 130
Great Masters of Scottish Football (Taylor), 55, 101
Greaves, Ian, 68, 154
Greaves, Jimmy, 18, 33, 62, 71, 83, 104, 127
  This One's on Me, 43, 48, 136, 170
Green Bay Packers, 233, 234
Green, Geoffrey, 13, 47, 112
Greenhoff, Brian, 114
Greenwood, Dick, 253
Greenwood, Ron, 57, 77, 78, 101, 120, 124, 150, 162, 201, 202, 221
Gregg, Harry, 19, 24, 28, 29, 39, 52, 176
Gregson, R. P., 92
Grundy, Bill, 212, 215
Guthrie, Jimmy, 139

Hagan, Jim, 137
Half Man Half Biscuit, 230
Halifax Town, 67, 120, 176, 179, 204
Hall, Robin, 230
Hamburger, Chris, 236
Hamilton, Billy, 24, 208, 254
Hancocks, Johnny, 59
Hand, Eoin, 69
Hanot, Gabriel, 58
Hapgood, Eddie, 134
Hardaker, Alan, 63, 159, 171, 185
  Hardaker of the League, 81, 142, 171
Hardman, H. P., 51
Harmer, E. W., 99
Harmer, Tommy, 24
Harris, Ron, 24
Harrison, Arthur, 248
Harrison, Dennis, 240
Harrow School, 86
Hartford, Asa, 25
Hartlepool United, 65, 182, 195, 204
Hattersley, Roy, Goodbye to Yorkshire, 182, 197
Havelange, Joao, 255
Havering Nalgo FC, 146

INDEX